ON ANY GIVEN SUNDAY

THE STORY
OF CHRIST IN THE
DIVINE SERVICE

By weaving worship education into the private thoughts of John and Jennifer, the author accomplishes something very important. He teaches about worship not merely in an historical way or logical or doctrinal, but in a dynamic way: what's really going on in worship and what it means for me. Doctrine is essential. History and logic are valuable. But the dynamic helps people to own their worship and to appreciate it ever more deeply and personally.

Pastor Bryan Gerlach
Director of the Commission on Worship,
Wisconsin Lutheran Synod

On any given Sunday, millions of Americans attend services expecting a worship experience. Instead of delivering a carefully choreographed experience, Lutheran worship delivers a carefully curated proclamation of Christ's Person and work in the Divine Service. Prof. Berg, through winsome story and accessible commentary, shows us that Christ himself is the center of the Divine Service. In it, Christ is both proclaimed and present. Blessed are the people at an ordinary church, served by an ordinary pastor, who – week in and week out - receive extraordinary Gospel gifts from the Savior!

Prof. Aaron Christie
Dean of Chapel
Professor of Liturgics and Homiletics
Wisconsin Lutheran Seminary
Mequon, WI

On Any Given Sunday uniquely reveals the happy marriage of substance and style – the *what* and the *how* – of liturgical worship. We immerse in the gritty struggles of John and Jennifer as Christ is drawn into their story, better, as Christ draws them all the way into his by the hidden glory of the Divine Service. The prose that surrounds their drama is Word-saturated and Christ-obsessed. I found myself yearning to take my bride to church.

Dr. Mark Paustian
Author of *Our Worth to Him*

ON ANY GIVEN SUNDAY

THE STORY OF CHRIST IN THE DIVINE SERVICE

MICHAEL BERG

FOREWORD BY: BROR ERICKSON

On Any Given Sunday: The Story of Christ in the Divine Service

© 2022 New Reformation Publications

All rights reserved. No part of this publication may be reproduced, distributed, or transmitted in any form or by any means, including photocopying, recording, or other electronic or mechanical methods, without the prior written permission of the publisher, except in the case of brief quotations embodied in critical reviews and certain other noncommercial uses permitted by copyright law. For permission requests, write to the publisher at the address below.

Scriptures taken from the Holy Bible, New International Version®, NIV®. Copyright © 1973, 1978, 1984, 2011 by Biblica, Inc.™ Used by permission of Zondervan. All rights reserved worldwide. www.zondervan.com The "NIV" and "New International Version" are trademarks registered in the United States Patent and Trademark Office by Biblica, Inc.™

Published by:
1517 Publishing
PO Box 54032
Irvine, CA 92619-4032

Names: Berg, Mike, 1978- author. | Erickson, Bror, writer of foreword.
Title: On any given Sunday : the story of Christ in the Divine Service / Michael Berg ; foreword by Bror Erickson.
Description: Irvine, CA : 1517 Publishing, [2023]
Identifiers: ISBN: 978-1-956658-10-1 (hardcover) | 978-1-956658-11-8 (paperback) | 978-1-956658-12-5 (ebook) | 978-1-956658-13-2 (audio)
Subjects: LCSH: Lutheran Church—Liturgy. | Public worship—Lutheran Church. | Jesus Christ—Presence. | Love—Religious aspects—Lutheran Church. | Forgiveness—Religious aspects—Lutheran Church. | BISAC: RELIGION / Christian Rituals & Practice / Worship & Liturgy. | RELIGION / Christian Rituals & Practice / General. | RELIGION / Christianity / Lutheran.
Classification: LCC: BX8067.A1 B47 2023 | DDC: 264.041—dc23

To the people of St. John's Lutheran Church in Wood Lake,
MN, my first parish.
You taught me more than I ever taught you.

CONTENTS

Foreword...xi

Prologue..xiii

Part One: A Story of the Divine Service 1

Part Two: The Life of Christ in Poetry and Prose.............. 67

Addendum A: The Church Year 113

Addendum B: Biblical Basis for the Parts
   of the Divine Service................................. 121

FOREWORD

In *On Any Given Sunday* Mike Berg draws on his many years of experience as both a pastor and a professor to illustrate the pastoral benefit of liturgical worship and its importance and purpose to the average Christian today. Ironically, the story does not take place on Sunday, but on a Thursday evening commemorating the Ascension, a service that uses the liturgy common to Sunday mornings. The characters have all too common experiences and issues they have to deal with in this sinful world, and then in the course of the liturgy and the readings they find that God deals with those issues for them. Of course, these all too common experiences and issues are their issues, and yet in reading the story they take the place of your issues. This is the beauty of fiction as a vehicle for gospel proclamation, a Christian tradition that is rooted in Jesus Christ and the parables he told, which in turn were built upon parables the prophets were wont to use even in the Old Testament. The story allows you to contemplate parallels with the issues you deal with and reflect on your own experience in worship. The story is simple in style and rather free of literary flourish, which would distract from the story Mike invites you to participate in *On Any Given Sunday*.

The liturgy is the real story here, as is shown in the second chapter, "The Life of Christ in Poetry and Prose." Here Mike shows how the liturgical structure of the Christian church is centered on the story of Christ as it is told in a very Semitic way. Hebrew storytelling often has a pattern of giving an overview of the whole story before flashing back to focus on a detail or two that have greater importance to the reader. We see this play out at the beginning of the Bible in

Genesis 1–3 and later in Revelation as seals are broken and trumpets blown, and each sequence builds on another and gives way to interludes that focus on events previously passed over. Here, Mike shows the reader how the liturgy provides an overview of the life of Christ every Sunday as the seasons and Sundays of the Church Year work to draw focus to specific events within that life and relate them to the Christian. It is then through this liturgy that Christ's life is played out in the Christian's life so that the Christian's life becomes the life of Christ in the world today. After all, the church is the body of Christ; the work we do as Christians is work that Christ does through us who are his servants. He is the Vine, and we are the branches. So, the liturgy, the Word, and the sacraments all work to make it so that we grow in him as he grows in us.

The upshot is the book does a very nice job of inviting you, the reader, into the liturgy so that your worship life will be enhanced and enriched. Pastors will find this to be of great use for topical Bible studies in their parish, or just a good book to recommend to parishioners who perhaps don't understand what they are doing as they go through the motions on Sunday mornings.

Your brother in Christ,
Pastor Bror Erickson

PROLOGUE

On any given Sunday, the story of Christ is retold with poetry and prose, music and lyrics. This narrative of Christ's life is called the "Divine Service." It is such a beautiful expression of the faith that countless Christians from across the globe, of every culture, from every class, and in every era, sing, chant, listen to, and read some of the same words every week. How mind boggling it is that Jesus said some of the same words we sing on Sunday, that Justin Martyr and John Chrysostom read some of the same readings, that Augustine prayed some of the same prayers, and that Martin Luther chanted some of the same chants! How astounding it is that a man in Beijing, a woman in Moscow, a boy in Nairobi, and a girl in Buenos Aries can share such an intimate connection through the Divine Service in an otherwise contentious world? This involves much more than conservative traditions clinging to old rituals or a repristination of some imaginary golden age; it is a special bond between Christ and his body. It is the story of Christ. It *is* Christ in Word and Sacrament. To understand the Divine Service is to understand how Christ encounters us in this world. I hope this book helps you understand this beautiful treasure.

It is amazing that many of the words remain unchanged and the basic form of the service has kept its shape. This is not because the church was so humble that it did not change much over the centuries. The itching ears of the first century (2 Timothy 4:3) are the same today and were the same in the Imperial, the Medieval, and the Reformation eras of the church. The Service has remained intact due to something far more potent than either stubbornness or conformist attitudes. It remains a static entity because it has its roots in the Jewish synagogues, its woody substance from the Scriptures, its strong trunk from the creeds precisely crafted during the controversies of the early church, its reaching branches from the musical talents of the laity, and its colorful leaves from every culture and language of the world. In short, it is a summary of Holy Writ checked and rechecked by generation after generation of the faithful to make sure all is accurate, all is beneficial, and all is beautiful. It is the path Paul marked out for us, "Finally, brothers and sisters, whatever is true, whatever is noble, whatever is right, whatever is pure, whatever is lovely, whatever is admirable—if anything is excellent or praiseworthy—think about such things" (Philippians 4:8).[1]

This "democracy of the dead"[2] humbles us as we think about the history of our spiritual mothers and fathers and how they worshipped. The Divine Service has weathered the storms of National Socialism and Communism. It has outlasted times of illiteracy and renaissances of human talent. It has persevered through persecution and poverty. It has stayed strong through movements like secularism and rationalism. And it will survive modernism, post-modernism, and whatever else comes next. It has anchored the church when falsity and corruption infected her. It has welcomed the talents of God's creatures and honed them to reflect the heavenly worship of the Lamb as best as humanity possibly can. There is nothing the Divine Service has not seen. So, when trouble arises, we can look back to the past to see what our forefathers have done. We learn from their mistakes, and we weigh their wisdom. More often than not, we find a question we are wrestling with has already been asked and answered. The Divine Service protects us from the wolves in sheep's clothing and from ourselves. It lifts us from depression and enlightens our souls. It curbs our enthusiasm of ourselves and nurtures our abilities at the same time. Above all, it gives us Christ for it *is* Christ, the eternal Word and the Sacrament of his body and blood.

The Divine Service has been attacked and criticized, chopped up and added to for millennia. The debate over its place and purpose in

---

[1] NIV 2011.

[2] G.K. Chesterton, G.K., *Orthodoxy* (Peabody, Mass.: Hendrickson Publishers, 2008), 43.

the church is a never-ending scrum. The discussion is a complicated conversation that has involved cultural, sociological, theological, and even political considerations. What is often missing in this necessary but sometimes ugly scrum is the sheer beauty of the Divine Service. I think of it as a symphony. Many parts come together not to recite a dry and tedious tale of a man named Jesus, but a polyphonic presentation of grace that engages all the senses (God's modes of operation were way ahead of the educators who promote the audio, visual, and kinesthetic categories of learning). He knows his creation and how he wants to interact with it. The Divine Service is more than a recital of doctrinal facts that occurs on Sunday morning. The Divine Service is not cognitive teaching about grace as much as it *is* grace. It does not just describe grace; it *gives* grace. It is here that the church encounters a theological consideration when trying to decide what worship is and what to actually do on Sunday mornings.

If our God is an aloof god who remains detached from this physical world, then it makes perfect sense that our time together might be described only as "worship," which would suggest that the purpose of Sunday is primarily our expressions of praise to an all-powerful deity. If our God comes to us in physical ways to hand us salvation, however, then this truly is his divine service to us. To put it another way, if we must reach God through our own spiritual enlightenment, mystical climbing, or decision for Christ, then yes, Sunday morning is about how to get there, how to reach into the heavens, how to bring the divine into us, and how to become better people. But if he is really present in tangible ways, then Sunday morning has a different feel to it. Things look and sound different, and we perform rituals in specific ways because we are in the presence of the Almighty. He invades our space as he did in Bethlehem during Augustus' reign. He comes and shakes things up in our lives with his thundering law and his healing gospel. The words "Lord, have mercy" and "Glory to God in the highest" come to mind. Surely, we thank and praise him, how could we not? But Sunday is about receiving more than giving, from a human perspective. Our giving plays a bigger role during the week, and even then, it is still all about "God for us" as he loves our world through our various vocations. The debate over liturgics is a theological one, whether the combatants admit it or not. It has to do with the way God comes to us and deals with us. It's about the incarnation, the means of grace, the cross, salvation, vocation—really every doctrine is present someway, somehow in the classic Divine Service.

For most of the faithful in the pews, the Divine Service is, at best, comfort food for the soul, the words and songs "we love to sing when we are with our Lord." At worst, the Divine Service is mindlessly rote: something "we have always done." The symphony analogy is apt. To many people, a symphony is misunderstood and therefore just boring music. But to those who understand its complexities, it is an insight into the beautiful genius of Beethoven or Mozart. Now consider something perhaps on the opposite side of the human spectrum: hunting. For many, hunting reenacts the ancient struggle of man versus nature but at the same time involves becoming one with nature, in a way. It is about camaraderie between warriors, a sport with many subtleties whose tension builds up to one big confrontation (if you're lucky that day). To others it is only a cold morning of doing nothing. The novice to the symphony may never buy season tickets, but he can appreciate its value and beauty with a little understanding. Similarly, a stranger to the outdoors may never spend the early hours in a deer-blind, but with a little understanding he can appreciate the value and beauty of the sport.[3]

So it goes with the Divine Service. An evaluation of the Divine Service isn't about our likes and dislikes; it is about understanding the church's reason for doing what she has done for so long. Herein lies the problem. Most do not know why the *Kyrie* is sung or what the word *Sanctus* means or why the Gospel Reading is the third reading from Scripture. Most have never been taught. I know I wasn't! The result of liturgical illiteracy is either a mindless slavery to tradition or an addiction to incessant change. The debate over what should be done on any given Sunday will continue and that's okay; it is even a good thing. However, in the midst of the melee, this beautiful symphony that accompanies Christ's saving actions is begging to be appreciated.

Before the cry of impracticality drowns out the sweet song of the liturgy, there are very practical reasons to learn about our Sunday morning heritage. For the vast majority of people, this hour on Sunday

---

[3] This is true even if one has moral concerns about a particular endeavor, in this case, hunting.

morning is the most contact they will have with their congregation, their pastor, and even the Word of God. This fact alone is enough to demand a thorough understanding of the nuts and bolts of the Divine Service. As mentioned above, a fuller comprehension leads to at least appreciation and even love. The Service is never boring; the sermon may be, but the Service cannot be. Heaven and earth are crashing together! Law is bellowed loudly, and gospel is spoken sweetly! There is nothing boring about it ... so long as people understand what is happening. So there is nothing more practical than to learn about our Christian liturgy of Word and Meal. Understanding makes Sunday meaningful. As we dive into the Service, we also discover a plethora of doctrines taught in a practical way, from original sin to the atonement. We also see the life of Christ laid out before us. It is a treasure trove ready to be explored.

Failure to explore these riches from the history of Christian practice can also have a negative impact on congregation members. In addition to ignorance, it results in apathy. If we do not understand what is going on, then we go through the motions mindlessly and risk becoming superstitious slaves to tradition without even knowing it. If we throw away that which we never took the time to understand, we only replace one tradition with another: our own. And this usually has a shorter shelf-life. To truly be well rounded and appreciative of all talents and ideas in the church, we must consult the past. Otherwise, we become quite narrow-minded.

The "these things don't matter" excuse is not valid here. Every church has a liturgy, and every church's liturgy portrays their distinct theology. From the Roman Catholic High Mass to the Spiritual movement of the Quakers, what a church does on Sunday reveals what it believes. You can't run from theology. So, since liturgy is important for doctrinal integrity and clear proclamation of theology to a congregation, there is too much at stake to ignore the liturgy. Therefore, the study of liturgy does not belong exclusively to the spectacle-wearing scholars in the library or to the musically gifted. It belongs to the laity.

This book is not an expert rendering of the Divine Service but rather a first step toward understanding the beautiful way God envelopes the church in his sacramental and saving ways. I hope that this book will be the primer you need to dive into the often-untapped treasures of the Divine Service. I am writing to a Christian audience and assume some biblical knowledge, but, like the classic Divine Service itself, the message of the gospel is proclaimed to all ears. My goal is to teach this magnificent heritage both to those who have scarce experience in a church building and to those who are regulars at church but never thought about or were never taught why we Christians do the things we do. I will tease out biblical truths from each part of the Divine Service and apply them to the Christian life.

Part One is a story. The characters are not important, nor is their story. This is not a full-blown novel but rather a short story illustrating the power the Divine Service can have on sinners. What is important is how the lives of the characters are taken up by Christ in the Divine Service. It is about forgiveness, love, vocation, and freedom. My hope is that this story of regular sinners who find hope in the Divine Service will find easy application to the lives of all who darken God's doorstep on any given Sunday.

Part Two treads the same ground but from a theological point of view. What does it mean to worship in the first place? What are we missing in our own context that was obvious to the average Israelite who approached the Temple or the sinner with whom Jesus broke bread? Why do we sing the *Sanctus* or the *Agnus Dei* and why at that particular part of the service? Two addenda are also added: a quick summary of the Church Year and a chart of passages relating to each of the parts of the classic Divine Service.

I should end this introduction with a caveat. This book is not intended to be an historical overview of the wide-ranging topic labeled "Christian Worship." Nor do I claim that my thoughts are the "way things ought to be" or that these thoughts even originated with me. I only speak as a pastor to troubled souls who, if they knew what was going on during the Sunday service, would be awed by God's arrival to them and deeply comforted that he arrives not with wrath for the sinner but with undeserved love. This is only one way of many to think about what happens in church on any given Sunday.

PART ONE

A Story of the Divine Service

Introduction

Most of the guards walked through the outer gate of Troy State Penitentiary with smiles on their faces. They laughed and joked with each other as they walked, almost ran, to their cars. It wasn't because their shift was over or because they were headed to their taverns or homes. It was that sound behind them: the heavy clank of the gate locking. After eight hours of the toughest work around, that clank meant everything. It meant freedom. They were on the outside and not on the inside. They left that hell behind them every day. Most of them knew that they were just a few stupid mistakes in life from being left on the other side of that clank: a side where the sound had a different meaning. The line between the guards and the prisoners was thin. Every day they thanked their lucky stars that they were on the right side of that thin line. Not so for John. That clank might as well have sounded for his life outside work. He felt imprisoned. Worst of all, it was a prison of his own making, and he knew it.

  A few years ago, John had finished a tour in Afghanistan. He had seen some horrific things, although not as many as others had seen. Returning home with both his body and his mind intact made him one of the lucky ones. He even came back to a loving wife and a warm home. There was only one thing missing. John had planned on becoming a police officer in his hometown, but he couldn't get onto the force. His humble dream of becoming a sergeant or detective had been ruined because of one mistake. A youth spent drinking too much and picking fights caught up to him one night. He didn't remember what this particular rumble was all about—something stupid, no doubt. He did remember breaking his opponent's nose. A night in jail was the penalty. It was this event that led him to join the army in the first place. When he returned home from the Middle East, the sheriff in his small conservative town wouldn't hire John because of his indiscretion; he had a long memory. The prison warden, on the other hand, was desperate, and John got the job.

John had felt a little emasculated by the whole situation. His frustration spilled over into his married life. His wife was a good woman; Jennifer stood by her man. She waited patiently as he fulfilled his duty to his country. They were both eager to start a family upon his return. They tried and tried but nothing happened for two years. It was hard for them to get excited about a vague possibility especially after so many disappointments.

John grew distant. He was too embarrassed to talk about his job or his infertility. The fertility doctor wasn't cheap either, and the financial strain added stress to an already fragile marriage. To ease the burden, John started working on weekends and so did Jennifer. John worked the third shift at the prison on Saturdays. Jennifer took every overtime hour available to her at the county's Children and Family Services office. It seemed like they never saw each other.

It was too much for John to handle. He snapped at his wife more often than ever before, hearing every complaint of hers as a criticism of his ineptitude and impotence. And then, one warm May evening, he did what he did. It was one of the worst nights of his life and he desperately wished he could start that day over, but he couldn't. It would forever be a part of who he was and who his wife was. He did more than yell at his wife that night when she went after him for his reckless spending. He screamed. He became unhinged. It scared him and scarred her. He didn't strike her but as they both surveyed the shattered picture frame he threw against the wall, he might as well have.

Jennifer was devastated, and John was riddled with guilt. "This was not the man I married," Jennifer sobbed to herself three nights in a row. She never told anyone what happened; she was too embarrassed for both of them. John shut down. His offense was too heinous for him to even comprehend.

Jennifer was from a fairly wealthy family. Not generational money but good money. Her dad was a respected lawyer. He took over the family firm from his father. They lived in one of those smallish sized towns where "everybody knew each other" but not really. It was big enough to demand four law firms, but Davis & Davis was the biggest and most respected. Her mother stayed at home before starting a boutique real estate firm specializing in older homes around the town center. She convinced herself that she worked to pay for Jennifer's college tuition, but the truth was she worked for the status and the pure enjoyment of something to do. The Davis family had belonged to the Presbyterian Church for generations. It was the wealthiest of the churches. The building was old but well kept. It was one of the symbols of the old town center. It wasn't the oldest place of worship in town (the Baptists had been there since 1815), but it was the most venerable. Conservative but not fundamentalist, it attracted the gentry class if you could call it that. Jennifer's family fit that mold. They went to church most Sundays, but serious theological insight was not a part of their regular conversations. Business, local politics, benign gossip, and Jennifer's future were the usual topics. Church was a part of the community, and the Davis's were a part of the community. It was as simple as that.

Jennifer followed the predictable path of her status; she performed well both academically and socially in high school. She went off to college to a small liberal arts school just far enough from home to be on her own but close enough to retreat back home once a month for some cash from dad and something new from mom, either for her dorm room or her wardrobe. She decided upon social work for her calling. Altruism was honored in her family, so her parents didn't steer her towards a more lucrative career. The hope, no, the assumption was that a husband with good earning potential would be in her future. Her career choice didn't matter to them, just their only daughter's happiness. The white-collar husband never materialized. Still, they liked John, even loved him. He was devoted to their daughter, and that's all parents can really hope for. That, and grandchildren of course.

Jennifer started her job at the county with the enthusiasm only idealistic youth can bring. It didn't take long for the realities of social work and the jadedness of her coworkers to wear on her. She plugged along through the early years. John thought her idealism would take her through a few more years, but that she would eventually break down, burn out, or fully morph into one of those nonprofit laborers who simultaneously loved the work of charity but despised the stupidity of those they helped. Jennifer was more optimistic, but she knew that she would not be a "lifer."

Jennifer's closest friends followed the more desirable path, at least from the perspective of her parents' generation and class. A few years in marketing or finance, an expensive wedding, a few years of "enjoying being married," children, purchase of a four-bedroom, three car garage home, and finally the move to part-time work, just enough to maintain both the joys of family but also the righteousness of being a working mom. She kept up as much as she could. Maid of honor in not one, but three weddings followed by a seemingly endless string of baby showers. She was fine with all of it, genuinely happy for her friends, but she predictably faded from that scene. Not only did she not want to have another conversation about the latest technological advancements in baby strollers, but she also hoped that she would never be the instigator of such trivial dialogue when her turn came. "Just think, my daughter will be old enough to babysit your kids for free when you finally have a family!" was the type of cringe-worthy comment at which she mentally rolled her eyes.

Not that she was a feminist, at least not in the activist sense. Her mother went through a youthful stage of protest and disdain for the establishment, almost a prerequisite for many her age before settling into an upper middle-class lifestyle. Jennifer respected her mom for that and learned a lot about the history of suffrage, equal pay, and beyond. Her rebellion was quite tame in comparison, a modest ankle tattoo and a few classes in college offered by the resident sixties radicals on campus. Jennifer could navigate both worlds—the heady conversations with her classmates in gender study courses and her roommates in the off-campus house she shared with the type of girls who paid lip service to the plight of women while they dressed for the Saturday football game and parties to follow.

She could still run in both crowds years later: the endless debate about laws making their way through the state legislature that would surely doom the good work the county was performing for struggling families and the weekends on the lake with the old gang from college full of boating, cocktails, and more talk about strollers. She was not one so easily pigeonholed. She was not the type to be jealous and then cover that jealousy with self-righteous indignation nor was she the type to lose herself in the shallow world of the upper middle-class and ease her guilt with talk about hard work and self-reliance. She was, however, as were many women her age, constantly bombarded with the thought that she had to be one or the other. How could she turn her back on those of her same gender who suffered injustices? How could she not, without regret, grab onto the comfortable lifestyle so easily attainable for a well-connected and well-educated daughter of the partner of the largest law firm in town? She did not resent her friends who chose one over the other; she resented the fact that she felt forced into this debate she had no desire to be a part of. She just wanted to be Jennifer. She just wanted to be *John and Jennifer*.

A week had passed since the incident. Jennifer wasn't scared of John despite his outburst. That was not the issue. She feared what John *could become*. She also feared what *she* could become. What would become of *them*? She genuinely felt bad about starting the argument. She took care of the finances. She was better at it, and they both agreed that big decisions were better made by her than by him. Her vile words were not really about money but only a proxy for her frustrations. She wanted to hurt him, and she had succeeded. Still, he was more guilty, at least that's what she concluded each time she replayed that night over in her mind.

John hadn't said a word to anyone in six days besides his commands to the prisoners. It was a lonely life. The clank behind him didn't mean anything anymore. There was no more freedom on the outside than there was on the inside. He walked, slumped over, to his pickup truck, watching his boots kick up the gravel. He couldn't bear to raise his head up any higher. As he blindly dragged his feet in self-pity, he heard a loud screech to his right.

"What are you doing, John? You're gonna get yourself killed!" a coworker yelled as he stuck his head out the window of his black Chevy Impala.

John looked up and raised his hand in apology. "Sorry," he mumbled. The near accident barely fazed him. He put his head back down, not learning his lesson. When he arrived at his parking spot at the far end of the lot, John lifted his depressed body into the cab of his truck and turned the ignition. He immediately shut the radio off; he didn't want to hear anything at that moment. He rolled the window down all the way. It was eighty-five degrees, and the truck's air conditioning didn't work. The twelve-year-old, faded blue F-150 rumbled the fifteen miles home. All John could think about was what he had done. He pulled into the driveway and noticed that Jennifer had beaten him home. He stepped out of the cab, dreading the next few minutes.

He found his wife fixing her hair in the bathroom. Entering stealthily past their bathroom door, he sat at the foot of their bed. John could see the back of his wife through the open bathroom door, but she couldn't see him. He started to take off his boots but only got one off before he buried his head into his hands. He sat quietly, not moving, not even thinking.

"We're leaving for church in twenty minutes," Jennifer said softly. The pain in her voice was more audible than her words. He didn't dare argue even though it was a Thursday night, and he was exhausted. John had forgotten that it was the Day of Ascension, and there was an evening service at St. Mark's. He quietly washed up and put on a clean shirt. He left his bride dressing in the bedroom and walked to the car. John sat in his wife's tan sedan as the air conditioner struggled to cool down the humid air. A few minutes later he watched Jennifer step through the front door, lock it, and gracefully turn to walk down the front steps, her dress swishing to the left and then back to the right. She caught John looking at her with what seemed like a faint smile. It was his first in seven days. Jennifer put her head down and walked to the car, unwilling to continue the eye contact. They backed out of the driveway without a word spoken.

Nothing broke the silence during the ten-minute ride to St. Mark's. Normally John would be fumbling from one radio station to the next complaining about the commercials and overplayed music. Now it was off. Jennifer was usually racing against the clock, frantically applying her makeup. Tonight, she was still. They both sat in dead silence. John's hands were uncharacteristically at the proper ten and two position. Jennifer held her purse upright in her lap as stiff as a proper southern belle with white gloves and a wide brimmed hat. They felt as if they were in a funeral procession. It just wasn't appropriate to say a word.

The couple pulled up to the flagstone building with twelve minutes to spare. This was the earliest they had ever arrived. Jennifer stepped out of the car faster than her husband. She kept five paces ahead of John as they walked through the parking lot. John took this as a rebuke but for Jennifer it was just about surviving the moment. Once they entered the church, her demeanor changed. She was peppy and friendly as usual, greeting everybody with a "Good evening" or "How have you been?" John simply nodded to a few people, not breaking stride. He headed directly into the sanctuary, sitting in the back. Jennifer followed a minute later, sitting on the outside of him towards the stained-glass window of Christ walking on water. A massive foot and a half of red cushioned pew lay between them. They could have been strangers.

The church was a little warm and fairly empty. John and Jennifer had the pew to themselves – just the way John wanted it. He stared blankly at the large statue behind the altar as the organist struggled through a Bach piece. It was a beautiful sculpture of the ascended Lord. John could see the blood from Christ's wounds even from the back rows. The head of Christ was titled slightly down as if he was looking at his confused disciples. The stillness of the sculpture had a calming effect on John. He was no art connoisseur, but he often thought he would have been if his life had been different. The moments in time caught by an artist can say so much. The video and live arts could never reflect upon humanity's struggles and victories like a skillfully carved bust or well-painted canvas, capturing a moment in time. Many thoughts came to John's mind as he gazed ahead. He was in an entirely different mindset sitting in that pew than he had been while sitting at the end of his bed twenty minutes earlier.

Jennifer righted herself. Church was no longer just a community thing to her anymore. She had left that behind when she left the venerable First Presbyterian Church of Troy and joined St. Mark's. Not that St. Mark's was better or that the congregation of her youth was full of shallow people. They had a decision to make when they got married, St. Mark's or First Presbyterian. Both of their families were a part of their respective faith communities, but John insisted on St. Mark's: "It's the only thing I want," she remembers him promising. "Everything else we will do your way." It was a blessing for Jennifer. She was forced to ask the question of herself, "Why bother? What does this faith thing even mean? Why should I get up on Sunday mornings and do this thing called 'church'?" She finally came to realize that this was about God *for* her. After experiencing a lifetime's worth of human heartache every single week in her job, she needed to hear that all would be okay. She sat in that pew a yard away from the man who was the source of her deepest joys and harshest pains, hoping for some good news.

The Bells and Processional Hymn

The ringing bells broke John's trance. He instinctively stood up and turned around as the organist played The Venerable Bede's famous poem, "A Hymn of Glory Let Us Sing." Appearing from the narthex were three teenage boys dressed in cassock and surplice, looking sharp except for the ragged hair. The tallest boy held the crucifix, eyeing it up to make sure it was straight. The other two boys flanked him with lit candles atop their standards. They stood at attention with the same respect as the honor guard John was used to seeing. The pastor stood behind them whispering last-minute instructions, which the boys didn't need. He had trained them well.

With perfect timing, the procession took its first step as the congregation bellowed out the hymn's opening line: "A hymn of glory let us sing! New songs throughout the world shall ring." John stopped singing in mid verse as the crucifix and torches passed his pew. A familiar sight, one he had seen a hundred times before. John had even carried the crucifix and torches when he was a teenager, but that night a chill shot down his spine. He saw the sacred, wounded head of Christ limped in his direction as if to say, "I did this for you, John." Time seemed to slow down as every little detail of the sculpture flooded John's mind. He could see the tiny nails pointing out from his Savior's hands and feet, the sharp contour of his Lord's muscles stretched to their limit, and the crown of thorns piercing his head. He felt like the thief on the cross who was promised paradise in the eleventh hour of his life (Luke 23:43).

The torches passed his sightline next. It struck John that they were real: real wax with real wicks, and real brass followers. The flames flickered uncontrollably. The ceiling fans were spinning fast on that hot May evening, and some wax had blown over the brass followers on top of the candles. John watched one drop of wax run down the follower, onto the candlestick and harden, frozen in time. It was as real and authentic as the teardrop that began to roll down his cheek. The significance hit him like it never had before. John's Savior was real. His death was real. His suffering was real. It was real because John's sin was real. This also meant that his forgiveness was real. Christ's death for the salvation of John's soul was not like the plastic throw away world in which he lived. This was something different. This was not the here today, gone tomorrow, self-help guru making the talk-show circuit gush. This was a real solution to a real problem. How fitting that the song the people around him sang was not an overplayed ditty on the radio either. It was an ancient poem. It was a poem that had proclaimed the same gospel to generations of suffering sinners just like him. For the first time in days, John did not feel alone.

John made it through the first two stanzas but was too choked up to finish singing the hymn. He laid the hymnal on the cushion below him and placed his hands on the pew in front of him. He leaned over, too emotionally and mentally exhausted to go any further.

The Invocation

Pastor: In the Name of the Father and + of the Son and of the Holy Spirit.
Congregation: Amen.

"In the Name of the Father and of the Son and of the Holy Spirit," declared the man standing in front. Jennifer's own loneliness disappeared like John's. She had been baptized into this same name invoked by the preacher. It was the same name that John had been baptized into at the font, which stood so majestically to his left at the entrance to the sanctuary. The couple shared something that went beyond this world. Jennifer's mother believed in infant baptism despite the fact First Presbyterian had members who waited to have their children baptized much later. Elizabeth, Jennifer's mother, saw baptism as an adoption. Often, she would stop at the font in their own church before they entered the sanctuary and remind little Jennifer that this was the place where she became God's child. Jennifer's appreciation grew when she started attending St. Mark's with John's family. Through those sacred waters, she received the right to stand in the presence of God that evening. It certainly wasn't her righteousness that gave her the right; her life was a mess. It was God who stooped low to pour water over Jennifer's head twenty-nine years earlier. Now Jennifer could say, "Abba, Father" (Romans 8:15) with confidence. She had the full rights of sonship (Romans 8:15).[1] She was an heir to this rich family's inheritance. So there Jennifer stood, shoulder to shoulder with her brothers and sisters. She was not alone. Everybody else could leave her: her friends, her co-workers, her biological family, but her real family—the members of the body of Christ—would stand with her no matter what happened, no matter what she did. Deep inside she knew the man to her right felt the same way.

John also knew this well, but he had to admit he was a prodigal son. His latest gaff was not his first. As he thought about his heavenly Father, he also thought about his earthly father. His dad was a big and strong factory worker. His oversized hands were calloused from the tin he cut day after day. He too had been a military man, doing a tour in the Navy during the Korean War.

John was the youngest, the only boy in a brood of five. His father was tough on his only son, never letting up on poor John, or at least that's how John remembered it. John Sr. wanted a better life for his child. He was disappointed when John Jr. didn't go to college.

The pushing aggravated John. It was frustrating to have an older father who came from a generation in which men knew only one kind of love, tough love. John responded in typical teenage male fashion and rebelled. The two butted heads more than once. At eighteen, John left home as quickly as he could, thumbing his nose at his father. They barely had a chance to reconcile before John Sr. died of cancer less than three years later. Not reconnecting with his dad sooner was one of the many regrets John mulled over on a weekly basis.

---

[1] The New Testament refers to inheritance in terms of "sonship." In the Roman Empire sons inherited the estate while daughters were grafted onto another family. Paul is not being patriarchal when he declares "sonship" to Christians (Galatians 3:26). Quite the opposite! He is declaring the full rights of an eternal inheritance both to male and female, free and slave.

The Versicles, Confession and Absolution

P: Beloved in the Lord, let us draw near with a true heart and confess our sins to God our Father, asking him in the name of our Lord Jesus Christ to grant us forgiveness.

P: Our help in the name of the Lord,
C: Who made heaven and earth.

P: I said, I will confess my transgressions to the Lord,
C: and you forgave the iniquity of my guilt.

SILENCE FOR REPENTANT MEDITATION

C: Holy and merciful Father, I confess that I am by nature sinful and that I have disobeyed you in my thoughts, words, and actions. I have done what is evil and failed to do what is good. For this I deserve your punishment both now and in eternity. But I am truly sorry for my sins, and trusting in my Savior Jesus Christ, I pray, Lord, have mercy on me, a sinner.

P: Upon this, your confession, I, by virtue of my Office as a called and ordained servant of the Word, announce the grace of God to all of you. In the stead and by the command of my Lord Jesus Christ, I forgive you all your sins, in the Name of the Father and of the + Son and of the Holy Spirit.

His youthful rebellion was also one of the things he would confess silently that evening after the pastor invited him, "Beloved in the Lord, let us draw near with a true heart and confess our sins to God our Father, asking him in the Name of our Lord Jesus Christ to forgive us." There was a minute of silence before the actual confession. The congregation had been taught to use that moment as a time to compare their lives to the Ten Commandments. John needed more than a minute.

As the confession began, John's head swirled with memories. Images of his father sitting in his recliner in front of the TV, a half-chewed cigar hanging from his mouth. Next, an argument with his sergeant in an Afghan field entered into his mind. Finally, he thought of that fateful night a week ago.

"Upon this your confession," the pastor's words broke John's train of thought. He had no time for guilt or self-pity. The absolution chased that all away. It was so abrupt, John thought. There was nothing between the "I'm sorry" and the "I forgive." He felt like David standing before Nathan with all his lust, murder, and adultery hanging out like laundry for all to see (2 Samuel 12). Nathan wasted no time forgiving King David and neither did the man up front waste any time forgiving John. Before John knew it, the minister's hand was outlining the cross reciting those beautiful words, "I forgive."

The Introit

P: "Alleluia. Alleluia. Clap your hands, all you nations, shout to God with cries of joy. Glory be to the Father and to the Son and to the Holy Spirit.

As Jennifer and John sang the introit, the pastor walked the steps to the altar of God. Jennifer couldn't help but think how majestic it was to enter into the presence of God. The crucifix, now up front, caught her eye. It was the blood of Christ that gave her access to the Almighty and all-knowing God. She was baptized into the crucifixion of Christ and came out wiped clean, dressed in her Savior's righteousness (Romans 6:3-6 and Galatians 3:26-27). Now she could enter the Holy of Holies without fear or apprehension (Hebrews 10:19). The temple curtain was ripped in two (Luke 23:45).

Her thoughts went back to the invocation spoken moments earlier. Never before had she wondered so deeply about those words. "What are we mortals thinking?" she thought. "What are we doing – asking the vengeful God of Abraham and Isaac to come here and be with us? Don't we know that he punishes awful people like us?"

Jennifer was right. It's ludicrous. Unless one is baptized, unless one is forgiven. Then the seeming boldness is not hubris, but confidence in Christ. "What a motley crew this was," she thought as she surveyed the crowd and recalled the frustrations of social work.

"A house full of prodigal children coming home after wasting every opportunity: college students coming home with nothing but dirty laundry and empty wallets. What a Father we have to prepare a feast for us anyway (Luke 15:30)!" The members of St. Mark's were present at the family reunion, ready to eat and converse with each other, as all families do, in the presence of their Holy Father. Nothing short of amazing.

The Kyrie Eleison

C: Lord, have mercy. Christ, have mercy. Lord, have mercy.

John's confidence shrunk, as it often does for Christians who live the yo-yo life of law and gospel.[2] The prodigal children knew they needed help, and perhaps they had learned their lesson since they cried, "Lord, have mercy! Christ, have mercy! Lord, have mercy!" This was an appropriate petition for John to pray. His life was in danger every day while inside the walls of the state pen: a threat Jennifer worried about more than he did. They were, like many Americans, only a few missed paychecks away from losing their house and home. And Jennifer had health problems too. She endured seizures as a child, a condition which still required medication. What would John do without her? He would be lost. John was out of the army now, but what if he was recalled? What are the chances of surviving two wars? And there was always that fleeting hope of having a child. John realized a lot was in the hands of his Maker. Lord, have mercy, indeed.

At that moment, John felt a kinship with ancient Israel, a feeling he had while deployed. Fighting in the Middle East, John felt as though he were living in the Old Testament world. It wasn't simply the Middle Eastern garb or the shepherds herding their flocks that

---

[2] The law accuses the sinner. It says, "Do this!" and it is never done. The Gospel declares salvation despite the sinfulness of the person. It says, "Believe this!" and it is already done in Christ. The Christian is devastated by the law's correct accusation but is relieved by the good news of free forgiveness in Christ. Free from the accusation, the Christian ventures forth in a life of love only to fail and be accused by the law. Relief comes again in the Gospel. This is what is meant by a yo-yo life of a Christian.

made him feel this way. It was the Middle Eastern sense of tribe, so foreign to the individuality of Western law and culture. It was the theocracies that operated so differently from the principle of separation of church and state he was accustomed to back home. It was the violence, the blood, the anger, the passion, that made him think of Sunday School stories about David and Solomon, Jeremiah, and Ezekiel. His cry for mercy was a cry for a Messiah to come and end this mess with a glorious reign of peace and prosperity. As John looked forward to Christ's return, he understood how Israel felt as they looked forward to that same Messiah.

The Gloria In Excelsis

P: In the peace of forgiveness let us praise the Lord!

C: Glory to God in the highest, and peace to his people on earth. Lord God, heavenly King, almighty God and Father, we worship you, we give you thanks, we praise you for your glory. Glory to God in the highest, and peace to people on earth. Lord Jesus Christ, only Son of the Father, Lord God, Lamb of God, you take away the sin of the world; have mercy on us. You are seated at the right hand of the Father; receive our prayer, receive our prayer. Glory to God in the highest, and peace to his people on earth. For you alone are the Holy One, you alone are the Lord, you alone are the Most High, Jesus Christ, with the Holy Spirit in the glory of God the Father. Glory to God in the highest, and peace to his people on earth. Glory to God, glory to God!

As if God the Father in heaven heard and answered the congregation's cry right then, they sang the angelic choir's Christmas carol to the shepherds (Luke 2:14). "Glory to God in the highest and peace to his people on earth," cried the people around him. The answer to both Israel's prayer and John's was the same – a baby. Jesus Christ was the answer to John and Jennifer's cry for mercy that night. This was how God would save their wretched souls and bring him peace and prosperity. The people cry, "*Kyrie eleison!*" and their God responds, "Jesus Christ."

"Peace on earth and good will toward men" stuck in Jennifer's mind. She had heard it many times and in many versions throughout her life. How many times were these words crooned on the radio in the month of December? She instantly became nostalgic, recalling his mother's cookies and the presents around the tree. She recalled the first Christmas she and John shared as a married couple. Those were the "good old days" even though Jennifer knew it hadn't been that long ago. It appeared in her mind as an old home movie, complete with distorted color and bad audio. So much had happened since then.

She remembered his mother's words; she was the theologian of the Davis family. "Christmas isn't about presents; it's about Jesus." She thought of the Christmas Day Gospel Reading, "The Word became flesh" (John 1:14). This wasn't about a cute little baby boy; this was about God incarnate. Christ lowered himself to wallow in our poverty, in order to bring us to the riches of heaven (2 Corinthians 8:9). This was Jennifer's life. Poverty was not a distant tragedy in a foreign land or a different side of town. This is how John, or at least John's family thought. John Jr. and Sr. certainly saw desperation during their tours but that was what they were fighting for, to keep this evil at bay. How easy it was for her friends and family to ease their consciences by either convincing themselves that poverty was simply a result of bad choices or by pledging an extra thousand at the next benefit dinner. Not so for her. It was her daily reality. And not so for Christ. He became poor. What a sacrifice this was. It was the only way. Jennifer's sins were fleshy and tangible. In order to get rid of them, her God became fleshy and tangible too. He came for us.

As if on cue, the angels' Gloria turned to the Baptist's sobering cry, "Look, the Lamb of God, who takes away the sin of the world" (John 1:29). Jennifer began to look past the wooden manger in Bethlehem to the wooden cross on Mt. Zion in the distance. She reflected on how January's cold felt harsher than December's, even though the temperature was about the same. Then, a seriousness came over Jennifer's nostalgic recollections, even while she was happily singing, "Glory to God!" This cute baby boy came to die.

The Salutation

C: The Lord be with you.
P: And also with you.

The authenticity of it all struck John again too. This was a real life and death matter. The life and death of Christ, and John's own life and death. The pastor turned towards John. "The Lord be with you," he said. "And also with you," John responded. He knew the Rev. Wilkes well. He confirmed John, buried John Sr., and married Jennifer to John. He liked him well enough, but he knew others didn't—his dad for one. It was probably his dad's fault more than Pastor's. Rev. Wilkes was fresh out of seminary when he came to this congregation of six hundred souls as the only pastor. John Sr. had not been one to listen to some young punk and couldn't keep his mouth shut. Rev. Wilkes had no room for error. John always felt bad for him, being under a microscope like that, but surely Rev. Wilkes had brought some of it on himself; nobody's perfect.

But at that moment those personality differences didn't matter. This had nothing to do with Rev. Wilkes. He stood in the stead of Christ. It had been Christ forgiving John's sins a moment ago. It dawned on John that the pastor didn't say, "Jesus forgives," or "I think you are forgiven," or "I hope you are forgiven," but "*I* forgive."

"There is a connection between Christmas and Sunday," John thought. God became incarnate. He came as a real flesh and blood person to take care of the mess humanity had created for itself. Why would he ascend heavenward and leave us all alone! He doesn't. He still comes in real and tangible ways. John's eardrums felt the voice of this pastor forgive him, he had felt the water that had splashed over his head decades before, and he would soon taste the Sacrament of Christ's body and blood. Christ still came to save John's soul in a real and physical way. It was authentic. It was real.

The Prayer of Day

P: Let us pray.
Grant, we pray, almighty God, that we who believe your only-begotten one, our redeemer, to be ascended this day into heaven, may ourselves dwell in spirit amid heavenly things, through your Son, Jesus Christ, who lives and reigns with you and the Holy Spirit, one God, now and forever.
C: Amen.

"Let us pray," said the divinely ordained minister whose lone job was to not be himself, but to speak the forgiveness of Christ. The prayer that followed was magnificent. It was remarkable to Jennifer that the same prayer millions of Christians would pray that very night and that had been prayed for centuries, was exactly what she needed to hear. She found comfort in knowing that many others stood in her shoes and that many ministers had comforted those people with the same gospel she was now hearing. Both John and Jennifer stood in other lands, among other people, as strangers in a foreign culture. John as a soldier; Jennifer as a tourist. They knew how small they were, albeit in different ways, and how big the church was. This prayer that they shared with so many focused them on what was to come for the next forty-five minutes.

The First Reading

P: A reading from the Second Book of Kings…
When the Lord was about to take Elijah up to heaven in a whirlwind, Elijah and Elisha were on their way from Gilgal. Elijah said to Elisha, "Stay here; the Lord has sent me to Bethel."

But Elisha said, "As surely as the Lord lives and as you live, I will not leave you." So, they went down to Bethel.

The company of the prophets at Bethel came out to Elisha and asked, "Do you know that the Lord is going to take your master from you today?"

"Yes, I know," Elisha replied, "so be quiet."

Then Elijah said to him, "Stay here, Elisha; the Lord has sent me to Jericho."

And he replied, "As surely as the Lord lives and as you live, I will not leave you." So they went to Jericho.

The company of the prophets at Jericho went up to Elisha and asked him, "Do you know that the Lord is going to take your master from you today?"

"Yes, I know," he replied, "so be quiet."

Then Elijah said to him, "Stay here; the Lord has sent me to the Jordan."

And he replied, "As surely as the Lord lives and as you live, I will not leave you." So the two of them walked on.

Fifty men from the company of the prophets went and stood at a distance, facing the place where Elijah and Elisha had stopped at the Jordan. Elijah took his cloak, rolled it up and struck the water with it. The water divided to the right and to the left, and the two of them crossed over on dry ground.

When they had crossed, Elijah said to Elisha, "Tell me, what can I do for you before I am taken from you?"

"Let me inherit a double portion of your spirit," Elisha replied.

"You have asked a difficult thing," Elijah said, "yet if you see me when I am taken from you, it will be yours—otherwise, it will not."

As they were walking along and talking together, suddenly a chariot of fire and horses of fire appeared and separated the two of them, and Elijah went up to heaven in a whirlwind.

Rev. Wilkes stepped to the lectern as John sat down. The First Reading was about the prophet Elijah (2 Kings 2:1-11). The chariots and horsemen of Israel swooped down and grabbed the prophet to take him to his heavenly home. "Oh, if only I could have an end like that," John wished.

As a young war veteran, he thought about his mortality more than most men his age. He had seen death, and he himself had killed during his tour. His actions didn't haunt him like they did others. Pastor Wilkes had talked with him before he left for Afghanistan. Wilkes spoke to him about the vocation of a soldier. It was not murder – what he did. He was doing his duty. Still, the idea of death was never far from his mind. Suicides were not uncommon at the prison. His father suffered quite a bit, and John didn't want to follow in his senior's footsteps, lying helpless in a hospital bed for two months. He felt a little jealous of Elijah and his caravan to heaven.

Of course, he reminded himself, Elijah didn't have it so easy either. John thought he was alone; what about Elijah? John recalled his Bible History lessons. Even after God's glorious display of splendor on Mt. Carmel, Elijah felt like the only one who believed. It is not glorious things that God uses, a lesson Elijah learned as he hid in a cave. It was not in the wind or in the earthquake or in the fire that the Lord came to Elijah, but in a whisper. No wonder the show on Mt. Carmel failed to yield a thousand converts. No wonder Jesus was born in a cave. No wonder an imperfect man read from the lectern. No wonder water, bread, and wine are used and not gold, silver, and bronze. What a comfort this actually is! "I'm a simple man," John thought. "I don't have a lot of money. But it doesn't matter. My God's forgiveness is not only for the rich and famous, the prestigious and elite. He is accessible to everybody." All that is needed is word, water, bread, and wine.

The Psalm and Second Reading

P: We sing Psalm 47.

Clap your hands, all you nations;
   shout to God with cries of joy.

For the Lord Most High is awesome,
  the great King over all the earth.
He subdued nations under us,
  peoples under our feet.
He chose our inheritance for us,
  the pride of Jacob, whom he loved.
God has ascended amid shouts of joy,
  the Lord amid the sounding of trumpets.
Sing praises to God, sing praises;
  sing praises to our King, sing praises.
For God is the King of all the earth;
  sing to him a psalm of praise.
God reigns over the nations;
  God is seated on his holy throne.
The nobles of the nations assemble
  as the people of the God of Abraham,
for the kings of the earth belong to God;
  he is greatly exalted.

P: *A reading from the Acts of the Apostles…*
In my former book, Theophilus, I wrote about all that Jesus began to do and to teach until the day he was taken up to heaven, after giving instructions through the Holy Spirit to the apostles he had chosen. After his suffering, he presented himself to them and gave many convincing proofs that he was alive. He appeared to them over a period of forty days and spoke about the kingdom of God. On one occasion, while he was eating with them, he gave them this command: "Do not leave Jerusalem, but wait for the gift my Father promised, which you have heard me speak about. For John baptized with water, but in a few days you will be baptized with the Holy Spirit."

Then they gathered around him and asked him, "Lord, are you at this time going to restore the kingdom to Israel?"

He said to them: "It is not for you to know the times or dates the Father has set by his own authority. But you will receive power when the Holy Spirit comes on you; and you will be my witnesses in Jerusalem, and in all Judea and Samaria, and to the ends of the earth."

After he said this, he was taken up before their very eyes, and a cloud hid him from their sight.

They were looking intently up into the sky as he was going, when suddenly two men dressed in white stood beside them. "Men of Galilee," they said, "why do you stand here looking into the sky? This same Jesus, who has been taken from you into heaven, will come back in the same way you have seen him go into heaven."

Jennifer resonated with the Second Reading. It was from Acts, the account of the Ascension (Acts 1:1-11). At no other point in her life did she feel like an apostle of Christ then when she heard the story of the eleven staring into the clouds as if to ask, "What now?" What were they to do now that their leader was gone? What was Jennifer to do now that her marriage seemed to be crumbling and her friends seemed to grow distant?

"Why do you stand here looking into the sky?" Jennifer imagined the angel asking her directly. "This same Jesus, who has been taken from you into heaven, will come back in the same way you have seen him go into heaven," the angel said to the eleven and to Jennifer too (Acts 1:11).

As the angel encouraged Jennifer and the apostles, she remembered the Ascension promises Christ had already given them. These were the same promises that had been repeated by the pastor over and over again. Jesus Christ would be with them to the very end of the age. He would send his Holy Spirit to teach them all things. He was going to heaven to prepare a place for each one of them, and of course, if he is going through all that trouble to prepare a room just for them in the Father's mansion, then he will come back to get them! Why should the apostles worry? Had Christ not already proven himself by rising from the dead? Did they lack anything? Why should Jennifer worry? Would God not give John and Jennifer a baby, if it was the right thing? Would he not bless them anyway, even if they couldn't get pregnant? Would he not lead them to reconciliation? Would he withhold forgiveness to either of them? Of course not! God had already proven himself to Jennifer too.

The Alleluia and Verse of the Day

P: Alleluia. And surely I am with you always, to the very end of the age. Alleluia.
C: Alleluia. Alleluia. Alleluia. These words are written that we may believe that Jesus is the Christ, the Son of God. Alleluia. Alleluia. Alleluia.

The Verse of the Day, "And surely I am with you always, to the very end of the age," reminded John of one of those promises (Matthew 28:20b). Every day his Lord was with him and not just in a vague way; he was there with his saving means: his Word, his baptism, his absolution, and his body and blood. With joy in his heart and without need of a spoken rubric, John boldly stood up to sing with the angels and his wife next to him, "Alleluia!"

The Gospel Processional and Gospel Reading

P: A reading from the Gospel of Jesus Christ according to St. Luke
C: Glory be to you, O Lord!

[Jesus] said to them, "This is what I told you while I was still with you: Everything must be fulfilled that is written about me in the Law of Moses, the Prophets and the Psalms."

Then he opened their minds so they could understand the Scriptures. He told them, "This is what is written: The Messiah will suffer and rise from the dead on the third day, and repentance for the forgiveness of sins will be preached in his name to all nations, beginning at Jerusalem. You are witnesses of these things. I am going to send you what my Father has promised; but stay in the city until you have been clothed with power from on high."

When he had led them out to the vicinity of Bethany, he lifted up his hands and blessed them. While he was blessing them, he left them and was taken up into heaven. Then they worshiped him and returned to

Jerusalem with great joy. And they stayed continually at the temple, praising God.

P: The Gospel of the Lord!
C: Praise be to you, O Christ!

John and Jennifer remained standing to hear the precious words of Luke's Gospel (Luke 24:44-53). On this special evening, it was read in the midst of the congregation. Jennifer loved the Gospel Processional, especially on Christmas Day. Rev. Wilkes always made a big deal about it in the Christmas Day bulletin. It was fitting that the eternal Logos, the Word made flesh, which tabernacled among first-century humanity, would now be read out loud in the midst of his congregation. It was perfect for the John 1 reading on Christmas Day, "The Word became flesh and made his dwelling among us" (John 1:14).

The slow and graceful yet deliberate movement of acolytes and reader from the chancel to the nave gave the Gospel Reading some extra gravitas than the usual responses and standing on that Ascension evening. The Readings had been building up, gaining momentum, and crescendo-ing to this point of fulfillment. The procession represented the moment of history when BC crashed together with AD, when the Old became the New, when ancient prayers were finally answered. It was the moment when all the world's culture, history, economics, and politics changed forever. It was the moment when God became man. It was the Gospel.

It fit perfectly with the day's selection from Luke's Gospel in which Jesus said to his apostles, "This is what I told you while I was still with you: everything must be fulfilled that is written about me in the Law of Moses, the Prophets, and the Psalms (Luke 24:44)." The entire Law, Prophets, and Psalms had pointed to this one man, Jesus Christ.

The whole plan of salvation was taken care of. God had planned it from the beginning. Moses and the Prophets laid Christ's life out. And so it was with John's life. The Father knew him before time. John recalled the passage tattooed on his heart in confirmation class through memorization, "For those God foreknew he also predestined to be conformed to the image of his Son, that he might be the firstborn among many brothers and sisters. And those he predestined, he also called; those he called, he also justified; those he justified, he also glorified" (Romans 8:29-30). Why should he worry? Everything was in place.

The Hymn of the Day

John and Jennifer sat down, and this time they shared a hymnal. The empty space between them had shrunk to a few inches. They sang together,

> On Christ's ascension I now build
> The hope of my ascension;
> This hope alone has always stilled
> All doubt and apprehension;
> For where the head is, there as well
> I know his members are to dwell."[3]

"If eternity is taken care of," John thought, "everything else falls into its proper perspective." He hoped his wife felt the same way.

The Sermon

As the hymn was ending, Pastor Wilkes climbed into the pulpit. It was a sturdy piece of furniture. "Solid oak," Jennifer remembered someone once saying. It made the preacher seem insignificant and unimportant. The words that bellowed from that natural amplifier carried more weight than any 200-pound man could produce. A canopy with a dove carved into its ceiling must have given every preacher pause as he climbed the four steps into the pulpit. On the front, visible to all, was a quote from some Greek men in the New Testament. "Sir, we would like to see Jesus," these men said to Philip in the temple (John 12:21). They wanted Christ; they needed Christ. The inscription was a reminder to every listener to never tolerate nonsense from their pastors. This was no place for partisan politics, self-help steps,

---

[3] LSB 492:1.

thundering law without a hint of gospel, or cute stories. "Sir, we would like to see Jesus," was the laity's check on the clergy.

That was never a problem for Pastor Wilkes. In fact, many complained that he rarely smiled in the pulpit or commented on the news of the day. "He's such a downer," "He's never inspiring," were some of the exaggerated complaints. Some had a tough time appreciating the gospel. They thought of themselves as too mature to have their time wasted with sin and grace talk. "Let's get to talking about how to live our lives," they would say. They were bored with the gospel.

This attitude frustrated Jennifer. Jennifer wondered if the complainers had ever lived. It was one thing to intellectually reject the gospel, at least that *seemed* reasonable but to be bored with the gospel? "They must have lived very dull lives." Jennifer and Pastor Wilkes had a special connection. Actually, it wasn't that special; it was special to her because she came to the church in young adulthood. Their relationship was different than the old-timers who were old enough to compare him to other preachers or those who grew up with him as pastor. It was different for Jennifer because he took the time to get to know her, to teach her to navigate all the eccentricities of his congregation. She wasn't enamored with him (he had his flaws); she just appreciated the man for who he was: a deliverer of the gospel.

Jennifer often thought that there was a bit of selfishness in the generation before her. She was spared the unhappy experience of having such parents. Her mom and dad got married late. They were vibrant but old-fashioned. They had their spats, but divorce never entered their minds. In contrast, many of Jennifer's friends had come from broken homes. She never understood how some parents could be so blind to their children's frustration as their families fell apart. She saw it in her friends' eyes more than once. "How could a parent's happiness be more important than a child's?"

Wilkes, although a baby-boomer himself, was different. He wasn't addicted to change as so many of his contemporaries were, playing upon a sense of rebellion and self-gratification. Nor was he ultra-conservative. Never did he ramble on for thirty minutes lamenting the liberal media or the horrors of the god-less politicians turning his Christian nation pagan. There was enough sin in his own people to preach against. In fact, Wilkes' sermons were an assault on the soul. Nobody was left standing proud, at least if they had listened, and nobody was left without the gospel.

"You want heaven on earth," he started abruptly. It was typical of a Wilkes sermon: get right to the point. He tried to take the words of God already spoken and bring them into his people's lives. More often than not, he succeeded in taking the grandiose concepts of sin and grace and making them personal. It was his gift (a good thing because he had plenty of other deficiencies). Jennifer marveled that her pastor could simultaneously speak to the youngest listener and to the most sophisticated adult. He was kind of like John the Evangelist, minus divine inspiration, of course. John's words "God is love" engaged both a wise philosopher and comforted a small child (1 John 4:8).

"You want heaven on earth, but you cannot have it," Wilkes repeated. "You want everything to run smoothly. You think success is defined by happiness, prosperity, and comfort. You think God a failure if your family bickers and your health fails. You think him a liar if money is tight and your looks sag."

John thought of his wife at that moment. She always wanted peace. She was the type to pretend that everything was okay on the outside, even when the inside was rotting away. "She did that tonight," John thought to himself. "She was bubbly and friendly to everybody as we walked in but wouldn't say a word to me the whole ride here."

John imagined his wife as a stereotypical 1950s mother serving dinner with a smile on her face. Even with three screaming kids complaining about the food and her teenage daughter urging her father to let her date an older and obviously more experienced boyfriend, this mystical creature somehow forced herself to smile and pretend that life was perfect. It was an attribute John once admired but now disdained, especially lately. "She was just as stubbornly distant as I was this the last week. Sure, I'm guilty in all of this, but her vanity doesn't help matters. She always wants more, a better house, a lakefront property, dozens of shoes, the best clothes." It made John feel like a failure because he couldn't give her those things. She wanted the perception of peace and success when there was none.

"You want to slip into heaven unscathed with as painless a death as Elijah upon the chariots of fire." With those words John remembered his thoughts during the First Reading, how he too wished for life to be easy. His plank-filled eye stopped staring judgmentally at his wife that moment. Paul's words, "chief of sinners" (1 Timothy 1:15-26), entered his mind with a sense of shame.

The sermon continued, not leaving time for John to sulk. "You come here wanting to hear that your life is going to be wonderful, that your marriage will be stress free, and that your country will always be the center of the Christian world. You want heaven on earth, but you cannot have it. You are like those eleven scared disciples looking blankly into the clouds, thinking, 'What are we to do now?'

"Perhaps they thought their Lord would stay with them," Wilkes speculated about the eleven. "Maybe they were thinking, 'This is it, Israel's time of glory!' Perhaps they were expecting heaven on earth. And maybe they thought their hopes were dashed as their Savior ascended from their sight. And maybe you feel the same way. Perhaps you think your Lord has left you all alone to fight that cancer, to care for your elderly mother by yourself, to walk through the tense halls of high school as an unpopular and lonely soul, to make a living in an unforgiving economy. Perhaps you too are wondering, 'What am I to do now?'" John felt like he was a medieval prince with his own court preacher speaking only to him.

"The problem is …" John was expecting more law, a bashing of his lack of faith, a slamming of his weak courage. He almost wanted it. John liked the slap of the wrist law and then a twelve-step program of how to fix his deficiency. Sometimes he was a glutton for punishment. Although it would have been appropriate to scold the crowd for their lack of trust, Rev. Wilkes skillfully turned to the gospel, "The problem is you have low standards. Make no mistake about it: it is your fault; it is a sinful condition, but you have no idea what is in store for you. This world and you, yourself, have dragged yourself down. You have no idea what heaven is. You think a perfect home of 2.5 children and two cars in the garage is heaven, but you have a marvelous family of billions of the baptized waiting to greet you. You think a fat IRA for retirement is a haven, but he has a city of gold waiting for you. You think a five-star hotel on the beaches of Mexico is paradise, but he has a room in the Father's mansion reserved for you. You think a cancer free body or lungs that need no help breathing would be just perfect, but he has promised a transformed body, like Christ's glorious body for you. You want heaven on earth, but your standards are too low. You have no idea what is waiting for you.

"No, heaven is not on earth. Heaven is in heaven and will remain out of reach until you die or you graciously receive the chariot's escort, whichever comes first. But do not fall into depression. Do not take the road of pessimism. Do not wallow in self-pity. Rather, rejoice in your sufferings. They are reminders, if nothing else, of something better. They force you to say, 'This ain't right! This is not how my creator intended me to live. He wants and he has so much more for me.' And he does, he really does.

"And with this viewpoint you gain something many people live without: the right perspective. How much easier is it to face the great battles of your life when you know heaven is just around the corner? How much easier is it to work hard knowing that eternal rest lies ahead? How much easier is it to burden yourself with others' problems when you know they will be lifted off your shoulders forever? How much easier is it to say, 'I'm sorry,' when you know your Savior's blood cleanses those sins? How much easier is it to die when you know you will live forever? It is a burden, this cross of Christ. It is, but his burden is light" (Matthew 11:30).

Wilkes finished his homily with some advice, "Do not forget your baptisms. It was there that you were given both this promise and this cross. You were marked as ones redeemed by Christ crucified. This means you have the promise of the heavenly kingdom, but it also means you will bear the cross because the fullness of your inheritance remains in heaven. Every day, wake up and be reminded of this cross. Every day, be reminded that you belong to him, your heavenly Father. Nothing can touch you, no fear, no depression, no disease, no violence, no hatred; nothing can take away your heaven. And as you face the trials of that day, as sin pulls on your coat, trying to drag you down, as the wicked world throws everything at you, and as you yourself stumble and fall, be reminded of that promise that will never leave you. Be reminded every day until that one day when you will wake up and the cross will be gone, along with the sin, the wickedness, the disease, and the heartache. It will all be gone on that day when your struggle is over, and your rest can begin. And isn't that exactly what the angels told the eleven gazers of the sky, 'Men of Galilee, why do you stand here looking into the sky? This same Jesus, who has been taken from you into heaven, will come back in the same way you have seen him go into heaven'" (Acts 1:11).

The "amen" never sounded so powerful to John and Jennifer as it did that night. "Yes, truly this was the gospel I needed to hear, amen," Jennifer reflected. How often had John looked at his life in a depressed way this past week? "Just get through this day, this week, this rough patch," he often said to himself. He had lost his perspective on things. He thought his happiness should come first before his Lord and definitely before his wife. The married couple was learning what so many wealthy and self-absorbed people find out: self-gratification is not a recipe for happiness at all. Their heads were not in the heavenly clouds as it should have been; they were on earth. They couldn't see with the proper perspective. They only saw wants and desires, their own failures and disappointments. Their heads needed to be in the clouds, thinking about heaven. Then, and only then, would everything fall into its proper perspective, a perspective of sin and grace, of heaven and hell.

They both felt tired and worn out after the short sermon. They didn't know it yet, but similar emotions overtook them. They were one flesh despite the bitterness they both harbored only minutes before as they sat so far from each other in the back pew. They felt relieved and calm. They had been forced through the gauntlet and came out alive and intact. It was an odd feeling. They were strangely confident but at the same time humble. They were joyful, but not giddy. They sensed that there was something much bigger around them. The petty little problems of this life faded from memory. They were lifted up above the earth, far above everyday problems. From this perch they gained that proper perspective which had eluded them the past week. The world looked smaller, and the coming heavens appeared enormous. And they as a couple would survive. They would never talk about their spats, but they were shared experiences. They suffered—at their own hands they suffered—but they made it through. Their love would deepen as a result.

The Creed

We believe in one God, the Father, the Almighty,
   maker of heaven and earth,
   of all that is,
   seen and unseen.

We believe in one Lord, Jesus Christ, the only Son of God,
   eternally begotten of the Father,
   God from God, Light from Light, true God from true God,
   begotten, not made,
   of one being with the Father.

Through him all things were made.
For us and for our salvation, he came down from heaven,
   was incarnate of the Holy Spirit and the Virgin Mary,
   and became truly human.
For our sake he was crucified under Pontius Pilate.
He suffered death and was buried.
On the third day he rose again in accordance with the Scriptures.
He ascended into heaven
   and is seated at the right hand of the Father.
He will come again in glory to judge the living and the dead,
   and his kingdom will have no end.

We believe in the Holy Spirit,
   the Lord, the giver of life,
   who proceeds from the Father and the Son,
   who in unity with the Father and the Son is worshiped and glorified,
   who has spoken through the prophets.
We believe in one holy Christian and apostolic Church.
We acknowledge one baptism for the forgiveness of sins.
We look for the resurrection of the dead
   and the life of the world to come. Amen.

The sublime feeling continued for John as he recited the Nicene Creed. "We believe in God, the Father, the Almighty, maker of heaven and earth, of all that is, seen and unseen," confessed the crowd standing around him. "We believe in one Lord, Jesus Christ, the only Son of God, eternally begotten of the Father, God from God, Light from Light, true God from true God." Those last words were his favorite. They were poetic and beautiful.

    This creed was bigger than John. It almost had a heavenly ring to it. Confessions speak about the divine the best way we humans know how. Because of this, creeds have an other-worldly quality to them. And yet, this confession of the church catholic, which John recited that night, was structured and precise. One could tell that it had been written in a sinful world. One could feel the struggle and labor of the church fathers as they delicately yet deliberately wrote, "Begotten, not made, of one being with the Father."

Bitter battles with heresy and the devil himself helped forge these words. John stopped in his tracks almost every time he spoke them. Pastor Wilkes required his catechism students to study the creed thoroughly in confirmation class. There was a lot John forgot from those afternoons, but the Nicene Creed stuck in his mind. "AD 325," Rev. Wilkes said. "That's when this creed started to form. It's older than your grandparents and your country. It's over 1,500 years old. And many people died because they confessed these words. When you speak these words, you stand up and confess with those who died for the faith. You stand with Augustine and Martin Luther and your great-grandfather and your grandparents and countless others who have walked before you.

"And you know why we confess these exact words?" Wilkes had asked rhetorically. "So we never forget," he had immediately answered. "So we never forget their battles. Many people tried to say that Jesus wasn't completely God, which means our salvation would be nothing because it relies on a mere mortal. Some said that Jesus wasn't completely man, which means his sacrifice on the cross wasn't real enough, and his perfect life was a sham. We stand up and confess these words, so we never forget who this Jesus is, true man and true God, our perfect savior from sin. If we forget, if we allow those false notions of Christ to enter our church, we're in trouble. Big trouble. We confess this creed, so we never forget."

John thought of the men who fought those battles. His military brotherhood taught him to respect the warriors who went before him. He would never forget the blood spilled for liberty, and he would not forget the blood spilled because of Christ's cause. All the more reason for him to quit whining about his own pathetic life, he realized. How could his problems compare to those who lost their jobs for their convictions? How could he compare his pain to that of martyrdom? How could he look at himself with honor when many of those men and women had pleaded, "Father, forgive them," as the flames roared at their feet.

Just as John was intrigued by art, he also appreciated history. He gained this appreciation from his father, who liked nothing more than to watch an old World War II movie. John wondered what people would think about the church of his day 100, 500, or 1,000 years later, if the heavens and earth lasted that long. John certainly had an opinion about the Roman Empire, the people of the so-called Dark Ages, the pioneers in the American frontier. The prejudice of modern man was baffling. Twenty-first century man had an opinion (usually a pretentious one) of every class of people in every time and in every place. But what would his offspring say about him?

It wouldn't be pretty. Biblical literacy was down. Attacks on truth were up. More money than ever was in the hands of the people, and yet church buildings were built smaller and cheaper. Tragedies were more frequent, or maybe just more visible. Perhaps the most glaring shortcomings would be the complacency, the self-absorbed attitude, and the apathy of the church. John had attended a few church meetings. He had heard the grown men bicker over the most minuscule matters. He had seen the soap opera of his parish unfold. Mrs. Schmidt was angry because new banners replaced the ones her aunt had made thirty years ago. Mr. McGuire couldn't control his anger because a new water heater was purchased even though the old one hadn't yet busted. They rarely got around to discussing matters of mission or doctrine. John wondered what future historians would think when they researched the minutes of the average American church meeting. What would they think when they found such pettiness in an era when Christianity's center seemed to be slowly leaving North America?

The Offering and Offertory

Jennifer felt a tinge of shame too as she passed the offering plate from John to the usher. Her mere pennies never seemed so small after hearing what she had just heard and confessing what she just confessed. Jennifer and John were actually rather generous compared to most. It was one of those things Jennifer's father instilled in her from the beginning. He was a community man. There was no Little League team he would not sponsor or cause he would not champion.

The cynic might see a lawyer receiving cheap advertising, but Jennifer knew better. Her dad really did care about his town. So he tithed, and he taught his daughter this virtue. Her first paychecks from the grocery store where she worked during high school had been tightly controlled by her father. "Ten percent into the plate," she could remember her dad say a million times, "ten percent into savings, and Uncle Sam will make sure to take his share. Your Lord, your family, and your community, they come first—and in that order."

It wasn't the purest of motivations, but what was? Later she learned that these offerings weren't really about giving to God. "God doesn't need your money," Pastor Wilkes once preached. "He's rich. He'll be fine without you help. Your offerings benefit you first. Your Lord is teaching you how to trust. Take a look at the offerings of ancient Israel. They were to give the first fruits of their harvest. That didn't just mean the choicest of animals and grain, but the first part of the harvest as well. A storm could blow over their crop, an army could roll through and trample their fields, but they still gave the first to the Lord, not the last, after waiting for the whole harvest to be safe in the barns. It's like burning your first three paychecks of the year, knowing that you could lose your job the very next day, but still trusting the Lord to provide. Like always, God graciously makes it about us, even our offerings."

The same concept was true for the offerings that didn't involve cash. The special offertory that night was sung by a duet. The music was beautiful, and the singers were talented, but the real gift was the Word of God they proclaimed to themselves and to their listeners. It wasn't about praising God as much as it was about God using those two songbirds to preach the gospel to his people. The duet sang a version of the forty-seventh psalm, the Ascension Day psalm. "God has ascended amid shouts of joy... for God is the King of all the earth; sing to him a psalm of praise. God reigns over the nations; God is seated on his holy throne... the kings of the earth belong to God; he is greatly exalted."

A subtle calm came over Jennifer when she heard the words of that ancient song. He is God over all the nations, over all kings. Can he not supply his church with what she needs? Of course, he can. Jennifer chuckled to herself with sad humor as she watched the usher carry the brass plates to the front. "Who do I think I am, as if the church of God, the body of Christ, depends on me and my money? It's his money, and I am only in charge of it for a brief moment."

The Prayer of the Church

P: Risen and Ascended Lord, you broke the chains of death with your death on the cross and resurrection from the grave. You now have ascended into the heavenly realms to rule all things at the right hand of your Father.

You did not leave the apostles wondering but sent angelic messengers to comfort them with the promise that you would return in the very same way you departed. Comfort us with this same assurance through your promised Holy Spirit.

Do not let us fall into apathy but move us to speak this glorious message of your reign over all things to the world. Remind us and those to whom we speak that you direct the affairs of nations for the betterment of your kingdom.

Teach the church everything we need to know to be your witnesses to Judea, Samaria, and to the ends of the earth.

Above all, comfort us with the assurance that you stand before the throne of God advocating on our behalf so that the punishment we deserve will never be laid upon our shoulders.

Hear us as we bring you our private petitions.

Ascended Lord, lift up our eyes into the clouds in eager anticipation of your return.

Come, Lord Jesus, come quickly. Amen.

John and Jennifer stood up as the Prayer of the Church began. It was a magnificent treatment of the Ascension experience for the apostles and for the church left behind. The writer skillfully wove together the hope of the second coming, the urgency of evangelism, and the comfort of the session of Christ at the right hand of the Father. It was a sermon in its own right.

There was a place in the Prayer of the Church for private requests. The writers of the Prayers of the Church did their best to pray for all the burdens which weighed heavily on the hearts of the faithful, but it is an impossible task. A minute of silence was observed for the personal pleas of the congregation. Again, John needed more time. He quickly ran through his standard prayer list: his mom in Arizona, his sisters and their kids, the nation, his comrades in the army, and oh, yes, and the salvation of the world. Then he came to what really troubled him, his marriage. On that May evening he did not simply pray for a baby, as he had during the previous months. He had believed a baby would fix all his problems, but it wouldn't, as any parent knows. Now he realized that there was something else going on in his marriage that needed fixing. John thought that perhaps it was God who had not allowed him and his wife to have children, perhaps not—the plan of the Father is a mysterious thing. He quickly dismissed the thought; who was he to peak into the mind of God?

It was John's pride that was messing things up. He remembered a lecture he gave her about driving too fast into the driveway, scraping the bottom of her car. Everything she did that wasn't perfect, he made into a federal case. In contrast, he acted as if his shortcomings were no big deal. Everything he did that lacked his full attention: spending too much money and time on the things that he loved, those things were no big deal. It was just his wife nagging him again. He prayed for Jenny, poor Jenny. "Have mercy on her, Lord. It is not fair for her to bear the cross of being my bride. Give her peace, give her stillness."

Jennifer's prayer was just as passionate. She wished she was a better person, that she could do more for those she served. She prayed mostly for them. She got into the habit a few years prior of naming in her prayers those she counseled and helped navigate "the system," Marcus and Angela. Little Connor and his mother, Lydia. Ahmed and Billy, Carlos and Beth, Betty, Luke, Vanessa, the list was endless.

Then the time was up, and Jennifer ended her prayer abruptly missing a few names. The pastor concluded the prayer, "Come, Lord Jesus, come quickly, amen." Jennifer thought all prayers should end that way, "Just come, Lord Jesus, just come, and come quickly." It was a healthy way to pray, "Please take us away. We are not doing very well down here, just come, come quickly."

The Prefaces

P: The Lord be with you.
C: And also with you.

P: Lift up your hearts!
C: We lift them up unto the Lord.

P: Let us give thanks to the Lord our God.
C: It is good and right so to do.

P: It is truly good and right that we should at all times and in all places give you thanks, O Lord, holy Father, almighty and everlasting God, through Jesus Christ, our Lord... who promised that wherever two or three come together in his name, there he is with them to shepherd his flock till he comes again in glory... therefore, with all the saints on earth and hosts of heaven, we praise your holy name and join their glorious song:

Rev. Wilkes faced the congregation and started over with the words, "Peace be with you." They were now entering a new portion of the family reunion: the meal. This family had gathered and conversed with each other. They talked about their forefathers, about their greatness and about their faults. They talked about their brother, how perfect he was, how he saved them. They had laughed and they had cried, and now it was time for the family meal.

Then the pastor said something profound. He invited the people, "Lift up your hearts." It was as if something big was about to happen. Maybe a special guest was coming to the meal or a surprise appearance by someone important. "We have talked about a great many things," the pastor seemed to say with the short preface. "We have heard and confessed our troubling sins. We have heard about the grace of God that is given to us without any strings attached. Now we will hear how this transpired. We will walk with our Lord to his cross and grave. We already heard about his birth in the small town of Bethlehem. You sang the angelic response, remember? It was the Father's answer to our cry for mercy. His answer was the baby Jesus in a manger. But that baby boy's cuteness never saved a soul. It would require his perfect life and his perfect death to redeem us from our captor, the devil. So let us now speak and sing the rest of the story. Let's hear how the Son of God rescued the world. Oh, and by the way, there is a special guest coming to our table. It is Christ himself. In fact, he is both host and meal. Lift up your hearts, because here he is, the God-man."

"Lift up your hearts?" John wondered. "Yes. Heaven and earth are about to crash together! The ascended Lord has not left his disciples alone but has come to feed us with his Word and his meal. It makes perfect sense. God became man to save us, and now he also comes in a physical way to hand us the salvation he earned." Once again, the authenticity of it all bowled John over.

John remembered a military chaplain once musing, "If our God is evangelical, and he is – he does not rejoice over the death of the wicked, he wants all to be saved (Ezekial 33:11)—if our God is evangelical, then it makes perfect sense that he is incarnational (John 1:14). Otherwise, we humans would be left to our own devices to reach into the heavenly realms. The pastor doesn't say 'Lift up your hands and reach into heaven all by yourself.' He says, 'Lift up your hearts, your depressed and devastated hearts, because God is coming to you. Lift up your eyes, here he comes!' Our God had to come to us because we could never go to him. And his becoming man, his incarnation, that's true love. He lowered himself for us instead of reigning above with lightning bolts and erupting volcanoes. That's truly evangelical.

"And if our evangelical God is incarnational, then it makes perfect sense that he is also sacramental. He came in the flesh so we bumbling human beings could see, hear, touch, and smell him. But we are a few war-torn countries from Palestine and a couple of millennia of history from the first century A.D. We weren't there at the cross, but our God brings the salvation won at the cross to this camp miles away and two thousand years later. He is the Word. He is the Sacrament. His words beat upon our eardrums. His body and blood are placed into our mouths. Oh, and he is the true baptizer and the true absolver too. He's here, and he's real. If our God is evangelical, then he is incarnational. And if he is incarnational, then he is sacramental. And all this is for your benefit."

John had visited with that chaplain several times during his tour. He was a captain in the army and had served in Desert Storm. It gave him instant credibility. There may have been more atheists in the rugged terrain of Afghanistan than in the foxholes of World War I, but those young men still called the feet of those who bring good news "beautiful" (Isaiah 52:7). They had been transported from their virtual world of video games to a place where they shot real guns and killed real people. The sacrament, the absolution, the Word: these were real. Just as real as the chaos around them.

John never missed a church service while overseas, although the chaplain's rounds were sporadic. During the long intervals in between the chaplain's visits, John made fair use of a pocket Bible given to him the day he left for boot camp. This was when he started to become serious about pondering the Scriptures. The small book had a fake black leather cover with a tiny cross and his name written in gold at the bottom. The inside cover had a shakily written note that was barely legible. It came from the arthritic hand of his paternal grandmother. She had died when John was overseas. He always regretted missing the funeral, since he was the only male left in that family. His ninety-year-old grandma had outlived her only son, John Sr.

John stayed focused on her even when the pastor continued the service with the third preface, "Let us give thanks to the Lord our God." Every year John's family had climbed into their Ford station wagon (they always had one, upgrading every seven or so years) and traveled the two hours to Grandma's house. They left after the Thanksgiving Eve service straight from St. Mark's and would arrive just before 10 p.m. The adults would sit around the kitchen table sipping hot toddies as Grandma shuffled around them preparing for the next day's feast. Nobody lifted a finger to help her, not even John's mom. Grandma wouldn't allow it—she was in her glory.

"Grandma was so unselfish," John reflected. "She never wanted anybody to help her out, and she never wanted to take any praise—even though she made the best coleslaw, turkey, and dressing. She didn't care about the thank you notes we grandkids mailed to her for the Christmas presents every year. She didn't care about the polite gushing and clapping when she backed her way through the kitchen door carrying a perfectly roasted twenty-pound turkey. Her thanksgiving came as she gazed across the old farmhouse table at her smiling family. She did it all for us." So did John's Lord. He did it all for his family. "The greatest thanksgiving is to simply receive," John thought.

"It is truly good and right," Pastor Wilkes reminded John. "It is truly good and right that we should at all times and in all places give you thanks, O Lord."

John had to admit this was true. "It is right to give him thanks for everything, especially sacrificing his Son. So that we never forget where our life comes from, we thank our God at all times and in all places."

This was the first time John had really focused on the words, "all times" and "all places" before. His worship didn't really happen only on Sunday morning in a stone building. It was in all places and at all times. "Even in the prison? Even in the bar? Even at his in-laws?" He was starting to realize how intricately intertwined his worship, his thanksgiving, and his life were.

The Sanctus and Benedictus

C: Holy, holy, holy Lord God of heavenly hosts: heaven and earth are full of your glory. Hosanna, hosanna, hosanna in the highest! Blessed is he, blessed is he, blessed is he who comes in the name of the Lord. Hosanna, hosanna, hosanna in the highest.

Jennifer's own thoughts were pulled out of the mundane and lifted into the heavenly realms when the pastor said, "Therefore with all the saints on earth and hosts of heaven, we praise your holy name and join their glorious song…"

Once again, this lowly congregation was singing with the angels, chiming in with Isaiah's cherubim, "Holy, holy, holy!" (Isaiah 6:3). Heaven and earth really were crashing together! Not only were John and Jennifer singing with the angels, they sang with all the saints on earth. The song was not yet sung in unison, but one day around the throne of the Lamb it would be in perfect unity (Revelation 4:8). For now, the heavenly song was out of tune because the holy church on earth was out of tune. The church militant was singing with all the saints of heaven, but they couldn't sing together down here.

John and Jennifer struggled with this frustrating limitation. Both sides of John's family belonged to St. Mark's for generations, but Jennifer was a newcomer. She grew up in a different denomination. After her engagement to John, Jennifer met with Pastor Wilkes and jumped through all the hoops in order to join as a member of the congregation. The instruction convinced her that it was the right move to join St. Mark's, but it hurt her deeply that she was not of the same Christian stripe as her family. She sometimes felt like she betrayed them. The strife hurt her family too—they didn't understand.

It was not until Pastor Wilkes pointed her to that line in the Divine Service, "With all the saints on earth and hosts of heaven," that she finally started to understand. "You do have communion with those saints who dwell and worship in other churches," he assured her, "as long as they are part of the Holy Christian Church, that universal and hidden entity defined by faith in Christ." Jennifer's family was a part of the church. They were faithful. They believed that Jesus Christ was their only savior from sin.

Wilkes reassured her, "You, me, or even the devil can't break apart the body of Christ. Not even the gates of Hades will ever prevail (Matthew 16:18). This communion goes beyond brick walls and denominational lines. You just can't enjoy that wonderful fellowship here. But what were you expecting in a sinful world? We live in this mess, and we plug along the best we can. When we get to heaven, we'll sing together, in perfect unison, all of us."

Ever since those discussions the words, "Holy, holy, holy," meant a lot to Jennifer. John often looked at her expression when they sang them in church. He did that night. An angelic smile lit up her face again.

"Hosanna in the highest" was the next line of the church's song. Once again John and Jennifer were in the life of Christ. John could easily imagine the rugged rock upon which the city of Jerusalem sat. He had seen similar topography on his military travels. He pictured a crowd of people from all over the world walking to Jerusalem for the Passover festival: Arabs, Romans, Lybians, Cushites, Babylonians, all part of a multi-cultural scene that could only be outdone by the throng around the throne in heaven. Slowly the crowd begins to stir. A ripple goes through the city as the rumor spreads, "The King is coming; he's coming today!"

As if they were there themselves picking up palm branches and taking off their coats, St. Mark's congregation joined their jubilant cry, "Hosanna, hosanna, hosanna in the highest! Blessed is he, blessed is he, blessed is he who comes in the name of the Lord! Hosanna, hosanna, hosanna in the highest!"

They were there in Jerusalem watching their King enter his capital city on the very first Palm Sunday. The organ was booming, the voices were loud, and if they had palm branches, they would have been waving in the air. Of course, this group of Palm Sunday worshippers had the advantage of hindsight. They recognized the irony that so many back then had missed: their mighty King rode on a lowly donkey!

It was similar to the song they already sang, "Glory to God in the highest!" Another angelic song that lifted the hearts of the church, but with a twist. The thoughts of the faithful turned from joy to a harsh reality rather quickly. The King had to die. No wonder he rode a donkey into Jerusalem. No wonder the Palm Sunday account often kick starts the Advent season. In her wisdom, the church says to the faithful at the beginning of the Advent season, "Before you get too wrapped up in the busy joy of Christmas, remember where we are headed, to Jerusalem." How wonderful! Our King has finally arrived on his earth. He has finally come to Jerusalem! How sobering. He comes in a manger. He rides on a donkey. Again, John saw how low his Savior became to lift him to new heights. As he sang "Hosanna," he knew some of the original Palm Sunday choir would be shouting "Crucify him!" a short five days later. He knew the glory would fade at the cross.

The Eucharistic Prayer

P: Almighty Father, endless is your mercy and eternal is your reign. Out of love you created us and everything which exists. In mercy you preserved the church in Noah's day with a flood. In grace you promised to bless us through Abraham's seed. With patience you protected that seed through the judges and kings of Israel. In faithfulness you repeated your promises through the prophets. And when the time had fully come, you sent your Son, born of a woman, born under law, to redeem those under law with a perfect and sufficient sacrifice which paid the price for the sins of the entire world.

Next, the couple found themselves sitting at the table in the upper room with Peter, James, John, and the betrayer on Thursday night. Pastor Wilkes had prepared the table while John and Jennifer worried about themselves and their future during the offering, just as Christ had made sure everything for the Passover meal was set that fateful week two millennia ago. At St. Mark's, the prayer of thanksgiving began. John could almost hear a Jewish child ask the question which marked the traditional beginning of the Jewish Passover celebration, "Why is this night different from all other nights?" John hoped to have his own son or daughter ask him one day, "Why is this gathering on Sunday so different from every other thing we do?"

The Friday Seder meal was a regular occurrence for Jewish families. It was a mini-Passover meal served every week. The main Passover was celebrated once a year. This cycle was similar to the rhythm of the Christian Church: a yearly Holy Week celebration and mini-Easter celebrations every Sunday. For both, it was more than tradition. It was the story of salvation, told and retold to tender hearts of both the young and the old.

The prayer Rev. Wilkes read was fast and furious. It was read at a normal pace, but it was full of information. The prayer recounted the great acts of God, not unlike the Passover prayers of Israel did. God's saving flood, the promises to Abraham, the deliverance from Egypt, the prophecies, and most importantly, the life, the death, and the sacrifice of his one and only were all included. The story of salvation passed before John. It was humbling to hear God's actions in history recounted. John supposed that a similar pause of reflection had occurred in the upper room as Jesus reminded the twelve of their deliverance from Egyptian slavery.

The Verba and Eucharistic Prayer

P: Our Lord Jesus Christ, on the night he was betrayed, took bread; and when he had given thanks, he broke it and gave it to his disciples, saying, "Take and eat; this is my body, which is given for you. Do this in remembrance of me."

Then he took the cup, gave thanks, and gave it to them, saying, "Drink from it, all of you; this is my blood of the new covenant, which is poured out for you for the forgiveness of sins. Do this, whenever you drink it, in remembrance of me."

Therefore, gracious Lord, we bow before you in thankfulness for your many and varied gifts: for Christ's redemptive death, his victorious resurrection, his ascension promises and his powerful reign at your right hand. Bolstered by your endless grace and Pentecost Spirit, we eagerly anticipate his glorious return.

Back in the twenty-first century, the Thanksgiving prayer was abruptly interrupted. The meal continued in the upper room on the first Maundy Thursday night, but it was different now at St. Mark's. When Jesus spoke those words that night, so different than all the other nights, he changed the Passover meal forever. No longer was it a look back to the Exodus and a look forward to a Messiah. Now it was a look back at the whole story of God's creation, especially the Messiah, the true Lamb of God, and a look forward to the feast of heaven. Everything had changed, especially this meal, when Jesus uttered those words, "This is my body" (1 Corinthians 11:24).

An "amen" stopped the prayer at St. Mark's that evening. The prayer was over. It was time for something else. It was time for those special words that changed this meal from a Jewish supper of remembrance to a Christian meal of forgiveness. "On the night he was betrayed," Pastor Wilkes said in a different tone, almost chanting. They were simple words, words Wilkes had said before, words that John and Jennifer had heard before, but they were always special. Heaven and earth were crashing together. Jesus was coming to the table as both host and meal. How could they not lift up their hearts now? It was thumping and swirling. Their Savior was here. It was terrifying, exhausting, thrilling, and exuberant all at the same time.

"Therefore...," Wilkes finished the prayer that had been interrupted by the Words of Institution. He told the rest of the story: the resurrection, the ascension, the session at the right of the Father. It was a beautiful recounting of God's plan of salvation—one John never grew tired of hearing. He was reminded of what his Lord had done for his people, including himself, and now he would dine with that Lord. It truly was a meal of remembrance, but it was also a meal of renewal and a meal of the future. Wine/blood and bread/body would be served here at this table, strengthening faith and giving forgiveness along the way. Soon, perhaps in a few days, or perhaps decades from now, John would share another meal with his Savior. At that meal, there would be no need for forgiveness or strengthening for it would be the Wedding Supper of the Lamb in heaven (Revelation 19).

The Lord's Prayer

P: Taught by our Lord and trusting in his promise we are bold to pray:

C: Our Father, who art in heaven,
  hallowed be thy name,
  thy kingdom come,
  thy will be done on earth as it is in heaven.
Give us this day our daily bread;
and forgive us our trespasses,
  as we forgive those who trespass against us;
and lead us not into temptation,
but deliver us from evil.
For thine is the kingdom and the power and the glory
  forever and ever. Amen.

John was then rushed off to the Garden of Gethsemane as the apostles had been so long ago. The Maundy Thursday meal was over. The apostles sang some hymns and then it was off into the darkness of the olive groves. There, they stopped to pray. Jesus told his companions to keep watch, to stay awake and alert. It didn't happen. He prayed, and they slept. At times John felt that same guilt Peter, James, and John must have felt that night. John was once a go-getter, full of energy and enjoying life. Now he just went to work, day after day. He had become his father: eight hours of work, three hours of television and beer, repeated five times a week. He even sat in an oversized recliner like his dad. John felt like he needed to do more: more for his family, more for his church, more for his country. He was sleeping while others were toiling.

He desired self-worth again. The moment he felt forgiven was often the moment he wanted glory. He liked it when strangers shook his hand and gave him a heartfelt "thank you" for serving. He liked it when his wife complimented his work ethic. He liked it when Pastor Wilkes personally thanked him for working around the church property. He liked being helpful. He didn't like it when he found himself slumbering with Peter, James, and John.

His Lord was preoccupied that night in Gethsemane. He came back to his slumbering crew a few times and woke up his weak students, but he had something more pressing on his mind. He was in agony. The cup of wrath was handed to him. In this chalice of poison swirled all the punishment the world deserved. Think of the anger God felt when adherents of Molech burned their children (Jeremiah 32:25), the rage he felt when the men of Sodom ganged up on visitors (Genesis 19:1-29)—the sadness he had endured when Peter said, "I don't know the man." The devastation he went through when Genghis Khan swept through Asia, the fury that built up inside of him when skinny bodies were slid into the ovens of Buchenwald and Dachau. All of it swirled in the cup of wrath now figuratively in the trembling hands of Christ. Those words Jesus prayed in angst meant so much to so many Christians, "My Father, if it is possible, may this cup be taken from me. Yet not as I will, but as you will," (Matthew 26:39). Christ took the cup of wrath, and he drank it to its dregs. The mess of the Garden of Eden was cleaned up by Christ in the Garden of Gethsemane.

The famous Sebastiano Conca painting of Christ praying to the Father as an angel hands him a chalice appeared in John's mind. "That chalice of wrath was meant for us," John thought, "but Christ drank it instead." He had first seen this picture in a coffee table book at Jennifer's parents' home. He remembered nervously flipping through the book as he waited to meet them for the first time until Conca's work caught his attention. Christ kneels and slightly leans upon a rock in the painting. His arms are stretched out as in prayer, and his head is tilted up. He is looking at an angel who has descended to him. The angel carried a chalice as if to answer Christ's prayer in the negative.

Thoughts of the painting calmed John during that anxious moment. He thought about that picture as he too uttered the same sentiment as his Lord, "Thy will be done." It was a strange moment for John to be calm, thinking about his Lord suffering, his Lord drinking the cup of wrath, the apostles sleeping as it all unfolded, but John felt relieved once again. He uttered the petition that night with more meaning than ever before, "Thy will be done on earth as it is in heaven."

"Luther was writing about me," John thought as he remembered Luther's description of the "Our Father as the greatest martyr on earth" because it was slaughtered by thoughtless repetition.[4] However, on this night, as he pictured the beads of bloody sweat that oozed from his Lord's pores, the petition came out like an agonizing groan rather than thoughtless rote.

John mused, "'Thy will be done,' means that I will no longer play God, dictating what I think should happen, but rather I will let his will play out. And this is no great sacrifice on my part. In fact, it is a great relief, for my plans have gotten me nowhere. His plan, the one in which I live forever, the one in which I am lifted to untold heights and riches, the one in which his Son drinks the cup of wrath destined for me ... it's a pretty good plan. 'Thy will be done' is an easy petition when you think about it." It is, even if praying for God's will means praying against your own.

The Pax Domini

P: The peace + of the Lord be with you always.
C: Amen.

The pastor turned around at that moment with a different kind of chalice in his left hand and a piece of unleavened bread in his right.

---

[4] LW 43:200

The flat wafer traced the sign of the cross as the pastor said, "The peace of the Lord be with you always."

The Lord had exchanged the chalice of wrath meant for these people with a chalice of forgiveness. It was the simplest and yet one of the most profound actions of the night at St. Mark's. The peace Jennifer and John had sung about in the Gloria (which seemed like a lifetime ago) was theirs. Not that their problems had disappeared in the past thirty-five minutes or that all the nuclear bombs in the world were dismantled that night or that the Knesset of Israel and the PLO decided to bury the hatchet in the short time John and Jennifer had been in church, but that they, both John and Jennifer, had forgiveness. They had stood before the great Judge, as scary a place as anywhere. They had knelt before the one being that controlled their eternity, and they came away with peace.

The *Pax Domini* was another absolution. The pastor, once again putting forth Christ to his people, was saying, "You are okay with God. He has had mercy on your undeserving soul. And it is through this body and blood, which I place before your eyes, that you receive this forgiveness, this peace, this love, this heaven. Here is a foretaste of the heavenly feast. You are no longer the Gentile dogs licking up the crumbs that fall from the master's table (Matthew 15:26). You are an honored guest (Luke 14:15-23). Come and eat, all of you together."

That peace of God was too great to hold in. It was not meant for John and Jennifer to hold in themselves. It was meant for them to give. It was a peace they should have had all along. It was a peace they would enjoy together again soon. John and Jenny together. This meal they were about to eat together was a good start.

The Agnus Dei

C: O Christ, Lamb of God, you take away the sin of the world; have mercy on us. O Christ, Lamb of God, you take away the sin of the world; have mercy on us. O Christ, Lamb of God you take away the sin of the world; grant us your peace. Amen.

As if the ups and downs of the night hadn't been enough, the organ produced a different kind of tune as it played the *Agnus Dei*. What a contrast from the *Sanctus* which had been belted out only minutes before! It seemed that the whole heavenly host was in the balcony singing, "Holy, holy, holy!" Now the mood was slow and deep. The suddenly melancholy congregation carefully sang, "O Christ, Lamb of God, you take away the sin of the world, have mercy on us."

The Palm Sunday crowd now became the Good Friday crowd. It was the same city on Friday that it had been on the previous Sunday. It was the same person who had ridden on a donkey who now stood with a crown of thorns around his head. They were the same people wildly waving palm branches that now pointed their fingers angrily or cowardly faded into the background, too afraid to claim allegiance to the so-called "King of the Jews." The poignant and sad *Agnus Dei* changed the mood of the whole congregation just as the mood of Jerusalem changed so abruptly during the first Holy Week, "O Christ, Lamb of God, you take away the sin of the world, grant us your peace."

They followed their Savior through the tight city streets, stumbling along the way. Feminine cries could be heard around corners and behind the pressing mob so sad that Pilate had caved to the mob's demands. Simon from Cyrene was tapped to help carry the tree of execution. The cross's weight was a large burden, never mind the quilt of humanity also laid upon Christ's shoulders. The parade struggled up the hill called Golgotha on the west side of Jerusalem. It was the same city he had entered with pomp a few days before that he now left in disgrace.

On the other side of the capital city lay the Kidron Valley, just below the temple wall. It was said that the stream of water running through it would turn pink as the blood of the temple sacrifices seeped down the valley. No longer was that horrifying blood needed because the blood of the true Lamb was being shed on the other side of Zion.

The nails, the sign that read INRI, the vinegar, the gambling soldiers, the weeping Marys, the spear in his side, the darkness, the earthquake—they all flooded John's mind as he sang the words, "Lamb of God." John the Baptist's dire warning at the beginning of the Service in the Christmas song, the *Gloria in Excelsis*, was now an ugly visual. It had come down to this. John had seen Christ lay in a manger, welcomed him to Jerusalem with palm branches, dined with him in the upper room, prayed with him in the Garden of Gethsemane. Now he saw Christ fulfill his mission. The devil, who overcame Adam and Eve by a tree, would now by a tree be overcome. The devil, who overcame John and Jennifer, would now by a tree be overcome. "It is finished," Jesus declared (John 19:8-30). And it was.

The blood of the Lamb of God saved John from the Angel of Death. The wrath of God passed over John and Jennifer as it passed over those Israelite houses in Egypt so many centuries before. The Passover meals of the Israelite nation had pointed to this very week. Now the Lord's Supper and the *Agnus Dei* would transport the church back to the very same week. "Forget about the glory of the temple for a second," the song seemed to say. "Let go of his Palm Sunday entrance for a moment. It all comes down to this cross upon Golgotha." The simple words "It is finished" never meant so much to John.

The Distribution

P: The body of Christ given for you.
P: The blood of Christ shed for you.
P: May the true body and blood of our Lord and Savior Jesus Christ strengthen you in the true faith until life everlasting. Amen.

The story did not end with Joseph of Arimathea and Nicodemus awkwardly taking down the limp body of Christ. Nor did John's night end with the *Agnus Dei*. They didn't have to wait three days for the resurrected Christ like the apostles. His Easter experience happened right away. He dined with his living Lord that Ascension Day evening.

It always fascinated John that Christ ate with his disciples after he rose from the dead. He ate with the Emmaus-bound duo (Luke 24:13-35), behind the closed doors made famous by Thomas (John 20:24-29), and with Peter and the others on the beach of Galilee (John 21:1-17). Now John would eat too. John always reasoned that Jesus was proving the reality of his resurrection by eating—after all, how could a ghost eat? John knew there was some truth in that, but tonight it was about more than speculation. This was for him. If this truly was the body and blood of Christ, and it was, then his Lord was alive. And if his Lord was alive, then he too would live forever. This was as personal for John as it had been for Peter when he threw off his cloak and waded to the shore to eat breakfast with his Lord.

Jennifer felt a kinship with Peter and the others, especially doubting Thomas. The rest of the body of Christ is never that far from the consciousness of a Christian. Jennifer walked in their sandals. She confessed their words. She doubted like Thomas did. She couldn't deny it. She wondered how a loving God could allow such tragedy in the lives of those she helped at her county job. She wondered how a merciful God could allow so many to fall into addiction never to find a way out of this prison. She wondered why God didn't stop the wars, the disasters, or the tragedies. She was a doubter too, just like Thomas.

As she watched the pews before her march up to the communion rail, Jennifer could almost hear the words of her Savior, "Stop doubting and believe. Put your finger here; see my hands. Reach out your hand and put it into my side." Thomas wanted scientific proof. He wanted to put his finger where the nails once pierced and his hand where the spear once sliced. He would not be satisfied with anything less. Was not Jennifer the same? Did she not question and speculate? Did she not want proof, scientific proof? As if the Lord of creation had to meet her burden of evidence! What a silly thought.

Jennifer used to picture Doubting Thomas and Christ with halos around their heads as Christ overly dramatically pointed to his side, looking with a crooked head at his doubting friend. It was a nice but a distant scene in Jennifer's imagination. The image in her mind had changed when she ventured into a church in Rome years earlier. Her parents had celebrated their thirtieth wedding anniversary with a European vacation and took Jennifer along. Her parents had given her this thoughtful gift while John was still stationed in Afghanistan. She could get away from the empty house. It didn't help all that much. All Jennifer could think was that she was now half the distance to her husband. Frustratingly close to the love of her life but still miles of rough terrain and impossibly solved global politics away. She ventured on her own one day wanting to give her parents some space; it was their anniversary after all. She wandered the streets of Rome as tourists do, with one eye on the sidewalk and the other on a tiny map of the vast city. She found herself in a fairly small and dimly lit church. St. Peter's Basilica, which she and her parents had visited the day before, had been much more impressive. Jennifer wasn't expecting much, but when she looked up, she saw a copy of Caravaggio's

"The Incredulity of Saint Thomas." It struck her. The hand holding her map fell to her side as she walked ahead, mesmerized by the painting. The almost passive and aloof Christ in Jennifer's mind was real in Caravaggio's oil. Christ grabbed Thomas's wrist and was violently pulling the whole man towards him, so close that Thomas's finger unnaturally fell into the open wound of Christ's side. Jennifer remembered how startled she was by the painting. It was so real and gritty that it was almost disgusting.[5]

Jennifer was about to eat and drink his Lord's own body and blood. The body that once hung innocently on a cross, the body Thomas touched awkwardly, the blood that pulsed through Christ's veins, the blood that dripped from the point of a Roman soldier's spear. These would now be in her mouth. Jennifer the Doubter was face to face with Christ, behind locked doors and shut windows like the original Doubter. Christ's words were for Jennifer too. "Stop doubting and believe. Eat my body. Drink my blood. I'm alive! Stop doubting and believe."

Jennifer felt a strong connection to Thomas and the others, not only in their doubting and fear, but also in their euphoria in the presence of the living God who says, "It's okay. I am alive." The moment of distribution was more than a history lesson. Jennifer dined with the disciples. She had an experience with the resurrected Lord. No, she wasn't an apostle, sent directly by Christ, but she was a part of this holy church, the unbreakable body of Christ. Nobody can break up this body. Jennifer recalled Paul's words, "There is one body and one Spirit, just as you were called to one hope when you were called; one Lord, one faith, one baptism; one God and Father of all, who is over all and through all and in all" (Ephesians 4:4-6).

Despite all the nastiness of the world and the nastiness of the church—and there is plenty of that—nothing can rip apart the body of Christ. There is unity, even if there isn't visible disunity. Jennifer communed not just with the handful of faithful members who happened to remember there was an Ascension Day service that night but with all believers. Time and space are not strong enough to sever this bond. She was communing with Christ that night. And with Peter,

---

[5] See Simon Schama's PBS series "The Power of Art: Michelangelo Merisi da Caravaggio (1571-1610) and *David with the Head of Goliath*."

Thomas, her grandma, and her father. There was a connection there, a connection that came through Christ. She really was singing with the hosts of heaven.

Jennifer remembered a story some visiting pastor once told. "There is an old Norwegian church outside the town I grew up in. It is a country church out in the middle of the fields. Still has about two hundred members. Inside this white building is a communion rail. It is a perfect half-circle, as if it was never completed. The unseen half was for the saints of heaven. Those old Norwegians couldn't see them, but they dined with them, with the whole body of Christ. You can't break the body of Christ into bits and pieces. Nothing can, not your pain, not your loneliness, not even death. Nothing.

"I know, I know, heaven remains in heaven. Your grandparents' ghosts do not haunt your church. And the wedding supper of the Lamb will taste better than dry, stale bread and Mogen David's concord grape. Think about the Israelites in the wilderness. What did they eat as they wandered in their own wilderness? Manna and quail (Exodus 16). I'm sure they grew tired of it. We know they did–they complained more than we do. But that miraculous food was what sustained them through the wilderness until they got to taste the milk and honey of the Promised Land (Exodus 3:8). It was a foretaste of sorts. They received miracle food in the wilderness, and they would dine like royalty in the Promised Land. So will you. You will eat the feast of all feasts, not your mother's pie or your grandma's fried chicken, but a real, royal, heavenly feast, in heaven. Until then, eat this miracle food, a foretaste of the heavenly supper."

Jennifer smiled as she continued to watch the people in the pews before her march up to the chancel. The organ was blaring "For All the Saints." It had a moving melody, which conjured up a feeling in Jennifer she rarely felt before. With a sense of relief she sang,

> "We feebly struggle, they in glory shine;
> Yet all are one in Thee, for all are Thine."[6]

---

[6] LSB 677:4

John knew his future was bright when he belted out,

> "But lo, there breaks a yet more glorious day:
> The saints triumphant rise in bright array."[7]

Jennifer couldn't help but long for the heavenly feast with the organ that loud and the meal that wonderful. Between the stanzas she could faintly hear the voice of the pastor, "The body of Christ given for you. The blood of Christ shed for you," as he went around serving each of his members. This was the throng that would one day gather around the throne to sing "Holy, holy, holy!" (Revelation 4:8). All that was missing now were the thousands upon thousands, the ten thousand times ten thousand of angels chiming in with "Worthy is the Lamb, who was slain" (Revelation 5:12). It didn't matter one bit to Jennifer that some of the saints before her could barely climb the three steps to the chancel or even kneel at the rail. These were the saints no matter how feeble they looked. And those three steps might as well have been Jacob's staircase to heaven (Genesis 28:10-22). Jennifer wondered what those old-timers were thinking as they climbed to communion. They were so close to that heavenly reality.

The usher finally reached John and Jennifer's row. John let Jennifer go ahead of him. They walked up the aisle, the ushers behind them. This was the last group to commune, eight in all. They knelt as they approached the wooden rail. The thoughts of the saints in the Bible and the saints in Jennifer's own family walked in her head. "What a meal," marveled Jennifer. Her mind went to her husband beside her. Somehow, she knew at that moment that everything would be okay between the two of them. Not only were they one flesh united in holy matrimony, but they were a part of the same body of Christ, communing together right then and there.

"The body of Christ given for you," Rev. Wilkes said as he placed the host on Jennifer's tongue.

"Amen." Jennifer replied. "Amen to all of it," she thought. "Amen to Christ really being here for me. Amen to forgiveness being placed in my mouth. Amen to the heaven I will receive. Amen to my doubts being squashed. Amen to all of it."

---

[7] LSB 677:7

"The blood of Christ shed for you."

"Amen."

Wilkes concluded, "May the true body and blood of our Lord and Savior, Jesus Christ, strengthen and preserve you in the true faith until life everlasting." It already had.

Back in their pew, John and Jennifer sat in silence as the vessels were covered. They bowed their heads in prayer. A humble thank you to Christ for giving up his life for them, for giving them his body and blood for salvation. "This couldn't have been scripted any better," Jennifer thought as she recounted Christ's life, his death, and his presence in the church. "His love is too big, his mercy too grand, his sacrifice too large for any Hollywood script."

The Nunc Dimittis

C: In peace, Lord, you let your servant now depart according to your word. For my eyes have seen your salvation, which you have prepared for every people, a light to lighten the Gentiles and the glory of your people Israel.

The organ switched modes again as the congregation stood up. They would now take a break from the story of Christ; or rather go back thirty-three years. They had been present at Christmas, Palm Sunday, Maundy Thursday, and Good Friday. They enjoyed their Easter experience with their risen Lord, dining with him at a special table. But now they would visit the temple at a time before the curtain guarding the Most Holy Place was torn in two (Luke 23:45), before the Lord flipped over the money-changers' tables (Matthew 21:12-17), even before he wowed the scholars with his twelve-year-old mind (Luke 2:41-52).

It was the fortieth day since the birth of Christ. The day Mary and Joseph presented their baby boy at the temple. It was the custom, the law actually, for the firstborn male to be presented at the temple. There the young family met a faithful man named Simeon. The Holy Spirit had once told Simeon that he would not die until he saw the Lord's Anointed One. That same Spirit had engineered this meeting, inspiring Simeon to go to the temple court that day. Simeon approached the holy family and took their baby into his arms. He confessed, "Sovereign Lord, as you have promised, you may now dismiss your servant in peace. For my eyes have seen your salvation, which you have prepared in the sight of all nations: a light for revelation to the Gentiles, and the glory of your people Israel" (Luke 2:29-32).

It was a bold thing to say. Simeon meant, "You can take me now. I know that I have salvation. I know that I have heaven. I know that I have life forever. What more do I need? It would be okay if a bolt of lightning struck me dead right here and right now. It would be okay if the Roman soldiers ran me over right here in the street. I have seen the Christ. I have held salvation in my very own arms. What more do I need?"

Those words were no less meaningful when they came from John's mouth. "I know that I have forgiveness," John thought as he sang Simeon's lyrics. "I know that I have heaven. What more do I need? They can take it all away, my wealth and my health, even my life. What more do I need? It would be okay if a car hopped the curb and ran me over as I walked out of church tonight. It would be okay if a prison riot took my life tomorrow morning. It would be okay if I suffered like dad. I have heaven. I just had the Christ, not in my arms, but in my mouth and in my ears. I have been given salvation. What more do I need? Let your servant depart in peace."

John's prayer of peace was indeed for his exodus out of this world, but it was also for his exit out of that flagstone building. As grand as the angelic songs were, as passionate as law and gospel can be, as awe-inspiring as this Holy Communion with Christ and his body is, there is a reality to the whole matter. On the other side of the old oak doors in front of St. Mark's is a world full of regular people, doing regular things day after day after day.

There seemed to be a disconnect between the glorious events inside of church and the mundane world outside of church. John lived with this disconnect but it never bothered him too much. He rather liked it, in fact. There was a sense of sanctuary in church. This was a rest and a reprieve from his regular day life. He never understood why anybody would want to bring regular-day life into the church–maybe those people were so much happier with their lives than John was. John appreciated that church was different. It allowed him to walk out of church with the thought, "There is something better in my future."

It was good for John to have his head in the clouds once in a while, thinking about his heavenly destination, something that he hadn't been doing lately. Yet he often missed the reality of God in his life outside those oak doors. His God was mundane. He was physical. He became man. When John tried to lift himself far above this world, when he tried to spiritualize everything, when he tried to drive a wedge between the spiritual and the physical, he robbed himself of the authenticity of grace which he had experienced at the beginning of the service as the crucifix passed his sightline. His Savior is real, which is a good thing because John knew his depravity was real too. If John ignored the fleshiness of Christ, then he ignored the gospel. If Jesus Christ doesn't come here and live in this mundane world John thinks so lowly of, then mankind is left to his own devices to reach God. And no Tower of Babel or skyscraper of wealth could reach high enough. John reminded himself of the famous axiom, "No Christ; no God. Know Christ; know God."

The Post-Communion Prayer

P: We give thanks, almighty God, that you have refreshed us with this supper. We pray that through it you will strengthen our faith in you and increase our love for one another. We ask this in the name of Jesus Christ, our Lord, who lives and reigns with you and the Holy Spirit, one God now and forever.
C: Amen.

John's bold prayer, "Let your servant depart in peace," was not only a prayer about heaven, it was also a prayer for his exit out of church and his entrance back into the world. It was about later that night with Jenny. It was about the next morning inside the prison gates. There was a connection between the peace of eternity and the peace of everyday life. John could go out into the world with peace in his heart because he knew for sure that he would be in heaven, so much so that he repeated Simeon's sentiments. He had everything he needed for eternity. The next few days, the next few years, the next few decades would be a whole lot easier.

A thought of his dad entered John's mind at that moment. His dad was wrong about occupations and careers. The elder John had been ashamed of his job and felt a bit bitter that he had fought so hard so others could make a lot of money. It took a while for John Jr. to grasp this. His dad wanted something better for his son–"This was why he was tough on me." Senior didn't want his son to be a factory worker like he was. He dreamed of his boy graduating from a big-time university. He wanted his boy to have a corner office with one or more diplomas hanging on the wall behind a big leather chair. It didn't matter what the job was, as long as it came with a six-figure salary and a little prestige.

Junior didn't have that same outlook on life. Not after his pre-marital counseling with Rev. Wilkes. "You are to be Christ to your bride," John remembered Wilkes speaking as the couple sat on an ugly yellow sunflower patterned couch in Wilkes' office. John remembers lifting his head and sitting up as if to say, "What was that?"

"You are to be Christ to your bride," Wilkes repeated. "He is the ultimate groom. And what did he do for his bride, the church?"

It was a rhetorical question. It was also harsh law. "You may think this an impossible task, and it is, but it is still your calling in life. This is your vocation, John. This is not only a promise you make to yourself and to Jenny, but it is also a calling from God. In fact, this has much less to do with you than you realize. This marriage is more about God and Jenny. You see, God wants Jenny to be loved, to be adored, to be taken care of, to be led, to be protected. And he has chosen you for the job. He is using you to love your bride. It's his love.

"And as for you Jenny, this is about God loving John. He also wants John to be loved, to be taken care of, to be adored. He wants someone to look after John, to support him when nobody else does, to stand by him when he stands alone. And God has chosen you for the task, as difficult as it might be. He is using you to love John. It's his love.

"You two are the masks of God. He has called you, John, to be many things: a son, a brother, a soldier, a citizen, a Christian, a husband. He has called you, Jenny, to be many things too: a daughter, a sister, a citizen, a social worker, a Christian, a wife. In each of those vocations he uses you to care for the world. He stands behind you. You are the masks of God.

"Oh, we want miracles all the time." John remembered Rev. Wilkes getting animated at this point. "We want bolts of lightning sent down from heaven to paralyze our enemies. We want a cash cow to appear grazing in our back yard. We want all of our diseases to disappear one day when we wake up. We want it our way, and we want it now. But God's foolishness is not our wisdom (1 Corinthians 1:25). He uses ordinary things to do the extraordinary. Think of the water of baptism. It is used to tear children from the grip of Satan and place them into the loving arms of Christ. Think about bread and wine. They are used to give you the forgiveness of sins earned on the cross. Think about me. Would you ever patiently listen to me for fifteen minutes on a Sunday morning speaking about anything else but sin and grace? He uses the ordinary to do the extraordinary. He uses you to protect this country, to love your families, to help troubled families. This is how he performs miracles. This is how he keeps the world running. This is how he loves. You are the masks of God. It is his love."

Senior was wrong about vocation. To him, it was about money and maybe a little power, but mostly about making a living. The more money, the better the job. If you had mentioned the word vocation, John Sr. would have probably misunderstood and thought about a week in Florida. For John Jr. it meant something different. It meant honor, or at least it should have. He had forgotten that during his walk of self-pity through the dusty parking lot to his pickup truck. Every job has honor. There is no shame in cutting tin because it's God's way of manufacturing. There is no shame in wiping toilets because it's God's way of keeping things clean and sanitary. There is no shame in changing diapers because it's God's way of caring for his children. There is no shame in guarding prisoners because it's God's way of keeping the community safe. There is no shame because the work is divine. It's God's work. It's his love. His idea of love and glory are different than ours. His love goes the way of the cross.

"And the flow of love," Pastor Wilkes continued with the soon to be newlyweds, "proceeds from God to you to others. It's like water. It flows downward, but it can't flow up. It can only be redirected. The love you receive from Christ is given to each other. God doesn't need your good works in heaven; he's got plenty, but your neighbor needs them.[8]

"Remember what the sheep will say at the last day? The Lord will say to them, 'Come, you who are blessed by my Father; take your inheritance, the kingdom prepared for you since the creation of the world. For I was hungry, and you gave me something to eat. I was thirsty, and you gave me something to drink; I was a stranger, and you invited me in. I needed clothes, and you clothed me; I was sick, and you looked after me. I was in prison, and you came to visit me.'

"And the sheep will reply, 'Lord, when did we see you hungry and feed you, or thirsty and give you something to drink? When did we see you a stranger and invite you in or needing clothes and clothe you? When did we see you sick or in prison and go to visit you?'

"And God will reassure the sheep, 'I tell you the truth, whatever you did for one of the least of these brothers of mine, you did for me' (Matthew 25:34-45).

"You don't love Christ by just loving him; you do it by loving others. The love of God flows from him to you to your neighbors. You receive that love through the means of grace. So may the love of God that is placed in your ears come out of your mouths as tender words and loving songs to each other. May the love of Christ that is placed into your mouths on Sundays make your hands and feet work to help each other. As the masks of God, may it flow through you to others."

John's thoughts jumped from that conversation in the pastor's study years earlier to the middle of the Ascension Day service. In the prefaces to the meal, Wilkes had prayed, "It is good and right that we should at all times and in all places give you thanks, O Lord, Holy Father." John had thought about that prayer. What did it mean, "In all places and at all times?" His memory of premarital counseling helped him sort it out. This event he attends on Sunday mornings isn't really about him "praising" or "worshipping" God, as if God needed the adulation of man to exist (a condescending theory of some atheists). No, John's life is a living sacrifice (Romans 12:1). His worship occurs Monday through Saturday, at all places and in all times. Sunday is about getting. Sure, he thanked and praised God on Sunday mornings

---

[8] Gustaf Wingren, *Luther on Vocation* Tr. Carl C. Rasmussen (Eugene, OR.: Wipf and Stock Publishers, 1957), 10.

and at other times too, but don't we all say "thank you" after getting a nice meal? God is like Grandma on Thanksgiving. He wants us to receive with joy and then get along with each other. The last thing on his mind is the need for praise. John received forgiveness on Sunday, and he worshipped on Monday by serving others.

The thoughts of John's wandering mind were very timely because the post-communion prayer was about to be spoken. Not only was this prayer a thanksgiving prayer, but it was a vocation prayer as well. John and the other members of St. Mark's requested that the love they received might be used in the world. John immediately thought about his bride. He had a duty to fulfill, and he was ready as ever to do it. It wasn't a pride thing; the doctrine of vocation took the work-righteousness out of John's thoughts. This was something bigger than John pleasing God or John feeling good about himself. This was God loving Jenny. John was simply honored to be a part of the equation—just as honored as he had been to fight for his country. It wasn't about him; it was about something much bigger. John now understood what his namesake meant when he wrote, "We love because he first loved us" (1 John 4:19).

The Benediction

P: The Lord bless you and keep you.
The Lord make his face shine on you and be gracious to you.
The Lord look on you with favor and give + you peace.
C: Amen. Amen. Amen.

John and Jenny had come full circle that night. After the "amen" of the prayer, they looked up and saw the statue of the ascending Lord looking down upon his apostles. Christ was looking at them that evening, and they looked back wondering what would come next. They had spent an hour with their Lord during which they were given everything they needed, including Christ's own body and blood. Now they would leave and venture into a scary and unknown world, just as the apostles did after enjoying their Lord's company for three years. It was a daunting task: to be his witnesses in Jerusalem, and in all Judea and Samaria, and to the ends of the earth, (Acts 1:8) to be a prison guard, a husband, a man, to be a woman, a wife, a social worker.

As if on cue again, Rev. Wilkes lifted up his hands in almost the exact position of the statue that loomed behind him. The blessing followed, perhaps the same exact words Christ had spoken to the eleven, "The Lord bless and keep you …" The Ascension promises spoken earlier came flooding back to their minds. Why should they worry? They had everything they needed and a whole lot more.

The Divine Service began in Bethlehem as the members of St. Mark's waited for an answer to their cry for mercy. It was answered with a baby boy in swaddling clothes. They had followed that boy up the craggy rock called Zion, now a man sitting on a donkey. They had dined in the upper room and prayed in Gethsemane. They had watched their Lord play the role of the Lamb of God, hanging limp from a wooden cross. They had eaten an Easter meal as Christ proved to them that he was alive. They had been so moved by God's love that they professed their readiness to die. Now they stood on the top of the Mount of Olives starring into the sky. Their Lord was leaving them. They would have to wait until he came back in the same way to judge the living and the dead. He did not leave them without instructions or blessings, however. They would turn their backs to the altar in a moment equipped to go out into the world as his witnesses, not only with their words, but also with their vocational actions. They would not have to wait ten days for the Spirit as the Eleven did. Every day was a Pentecost Day for them. The field was ripe for the harvest.

Conclusion

John's eyes were bloodshot and droopy as he watched those in front of him pass by his back pew. Jennifer too was tired not just from her long day or the nights of little sleep a hurt woman endures but because of the service. The Divine Service could be an exhausting and passionate experience. It wasn't always that way. And that was okay. The work of God does not depend on the emotions of man— what a disaster that would be! There were times when the hymns dragged and the sermon bored, but there were also times when the service leaves the listener feeling like a boxer after ten grueling rounds. That night was one of those times. John grinned slightly as he and Jenny were ushered out of their pew. He shook hands with the usher and the pastor, bobbing his head at each. It was an expression of gratitude, relief, and satisfaction all at once. He needed something that night. He needed the Divine Service. John needed Christ to invade his life, and he had done just that. He came as Word and Meal, and he shook things up. Jennifer received what she came for. She needed to be told that it all would be okay. She could not see the happy ending, but she knew it was there. Her Lord had come again to tell her exactly that.

They would be back again. They were relieved from all depression and released from all punishment of sin, but they knew their hearts. They would be back with guilt. So goes the life of an honest Christian. But it was not as melancholy as it might sound. They knew from where their salvation came. They knew from where true love came. They knew where their home was. Pastor Wilkes had one of those sayings, a corny old man phrase he repeated so often that people stopped listening but would somehow pop into their minds exactly the moment they needed it. "You can't stop the world from sinning, just as much as you can't stop it from spinning, but you do know where to find the forgiveness needed and the promise of restoration."

John and Jenny had a better life than most. They had peace, real peace. The peace the angels sang about. They left St. Mark's with that peace in their heart. The air felt cool and crisp as John and his wife stepped outside, a big relief from the sweltering heat in which they had arrived. John and Jennifer climbed into their sedan and pulled away from the church. They drove in silence once again, but this time it was a calm silence of reflection and not the dreary pall that had hung over them an hour before. Jennifer put her hand down where John's lay on the console between them, her pinky overlapping his. He glanced down to see the sparkle of the small diamond he had purchased years earlier. He remembered that day as if it were yesterday. Never had a man been so happy to give his very last penny away for a simple rock. "I love you," his bride said softly, barely audible to the human ear. He knew what her words meant. It meant, "I forgive you."

The next day the clank at the end of John's shift carried a whole new meaning. He didn't dwell about his night in jail long ago, his freedom from work, or that dirty prison. He thought about his freedom from sin. He would never again walk away from that clank without a smile on his face, no matter what devastation entered his life. He was free, truly free.

PART TWO

The Life of Christ in Poetry and Prose

A Grand Painting

Imagine that you are visiting the Uffizi Gallery in Florence or any other magnificent art museum. You have wandered around for hours overly stimulated by all the wonders. After a while, you find yourself before Leonardo da Vinci's "Annunciation" or any other famous work of art that comes to mind. People gather around the painting quietly. All is silent except the rhythm of snapping cameras and shuffling feet. People come and go, but the crowd seems to remain the same: part curious tourist, part artist looking for inspiration, and part art-enthusiast checking off a box on her bucket-list. Now imagine the museum's curator approaching you. In front of the whole crowd, the curator hands you a brush and says, "Go ahead. Add your interpretation, your thoughts, your talent." She removes the red velvet rope between the painting and the masses and invites you again, "Add something to this ancient and beautiful painting that has spoken to so many minds and moved so many souls. Go ahead. It would be our honor if you would do so. We just have one rule. You only get a brush stroke."

The heritage of Christian worship is like this mural. It is a magnificent painting. Crowds have gathered. Some are curious; some wonder at the talent of the artists and the craft of the art itself. But many stay to take in the whole scene. Their souls are moved. The painting depicts the story of man: paradise lost, and paradise regained. It is the story of sin and grace, of death and resurrection. It is the story of Christ, his life in poetry and prose. The mural is large and diverse.

You are not the first person to receive such an honor from the curator. Generations of artists, poets, theologians, and musicians have added their talents, expertise, theological insight, and passion to this mural. But only a brush stroke.

You are more than honored when the curator hands you the paint brush; you are awed. You stand before generations of Christians, some who gave their lives for this cause. The last thing you would do is roll white primer on the ancient mural, covering up the masterpiece so you can start over with a blank canvas. Think of what would be lost if you did that? What arrogance! What close-mindedness! Do these fathers and mothers not have something to say to me? And yet the honor has been bestowed. And it is an honor. An honor that spurs you on to appreciate the history, the theological depth, and the artistry. You take up the cause not as a tourist passing through quickly or even an enthusiast only concerned with the craft, but as a soul that has been profoundly affected by the painting. You are not the first nor the last with such an honor. This honor actually makes you feel small because so many others have had the honor. The honor has been given to every generation, to every era, to every land. Everybody gets a brush stroke … but only one.

The classic Divine Service is at once diverse and singularly focused. It both spurs on creativity and curbs enthusiasm. It is a remarkable work of art that is unparalleled in the history of mankind. What other entity claims to have roots in so many different cultures? What other entity has remained so static while encouraging new forms? We noted it before, but it bears repeating: a boy in Mexico City and a woman in Montreal, a girl in Seoul and a man in Nairobi are able to share the same prayers, hymns, and readings while also sharing, yes, sharing, in their diverse works of art, their own brush stroke that adds to the painting. But only one brush stroke. What could be more diverse? At the same time, this heritage helpfully curbs our enthusiasm as we contemplate the talents and treasures, but also the baggage we bring to the liturgical table. All things are made captive to Christ. It is ours individually and ours collectively. It is both humbling and full of honor.

From Eden to Eden

This heritage that is ours individually and ours collectively began in Eden with our first parents. And it ends with redemption in Christ, which results in the new Eden to which all are invited. The first church service occurred in a garden in Eden. There were two trees. One tree was called the Tree of Life. The other was called the Tree of the Knowledge of Good and Evil. These trees served as an altar of sorts. There was a preacher who invited them to eat from the Tree of Life but commanded them not to eat from the other tree. It wasn't just law preaching. It was a gift. Eat. But it was also a call to faith, "Trust me. Take me at my word. I am protecting you. There are some matters you cannot understand and do not need to understand. Be still. Trust. Trust me."

Do you see how this is worship? Worship is finally faith.[1] It is trust. We come into the presence of God and trust that he, as our Father, will not blow us away but rather show us love. We come to dine with him, to break bread with him, to have fellowship with him. We eat. And we listen. We listen to his Word. We listen to preaching. We take him at his word. It is trust. All the components of worship are laid out in the Garden: entering the presence of God, communing with God, preaching, eating, and trust.

No wonder then that the devil attacks worship from the very beginning. He wants to attack faith. Worship correctly understood is primarily a one-way street. The arrow is pointing down. This is not about our response to God (as we too often narrowly define worship) but about the gift. Sure, we respond with thanksgiving, but it is always about the gift. Adam and Eve entered the "worship service" with no other intention but to receive from God. Their thanks and praise were not the point. But along came the devil and said, "But it should be about you. It should be about your actions and your knowledge and your talents. Go ahead and eat but eat on your own terms for your benefit, for the knowledge of good and evil, to be God-like." And ever since that fall, man has been tempted to be the center of worship … as if he were God. We often fail to ask the question, "What is God like?" in favor of "What do we like?" as we choose a style of worship

---
[1] LW 36:291-293.

or a church to visit on Sunday morning. We make the same mistake our first parents did. We act as if worship/trust was about our action and not about God's actions for us.

Eden is restored despite this arrogance. The devil destroys worship, and Christ restores it. Christ's Revelation to St. John is just that, a picture of the heavenly worship. It is Eden again. So, it makes sense then that the church militant (still fighting here on earth) would mirror, in a way, the worship of the church triumphant (those already in heaven). We dine at the Wedding Supper of the Lamb (Revelation 19:9). We gather round the altar and the throne of the Lamb (Revelation 7:9). We even sing the same songs, "Alleluia" (Revelation 19:1-18), "Worthy is the Lamb" (Revelation 5:12), and "Holy, Holy, Holy" (Revelation 4:8). And we sing them in perfect unison with the multitudes who have come from the great tribulation from every tribe and people (Revelation 7:14). Christian worship is what it has always been, the most diverse endeavor in the history of mankind. Why? Because it is the earthly picture of the heavenly and eternal reality that every nation and tribe rallies around the banner of Christ, that every knee will bow and that every tongue will confess (Philippians 2:9-11). It is the amazing reality that those who bend the knee trust and confess in faith rather than fear and horror, that we will all be one despite the strife, hatred, division, and sin of this world. Yes, a boy in Mexico City and a woman in Montreal… Until then, here on earth, everybody gets a brush stroke … but only one.

We All Worship

There is something primitive about worship. Not in an evolutionary sense but in a Genesis sense. It is who we are because it is the way God made us. We are worshipers. All of us. Atheist and religious alike, we all worship. This is not only a Christian assertion but a broader, anthropological assertion. Many thinkers, atheist and religious alike, understand that man is *homo liturgicus*.[2] You have, no doubt, heard

---

[2] See James K.A. Smith, *You Are What You Love* (Grand Rapids, MI: Brazos Press, 2016), *On the Road with Saint Augustine* (Grand Rapids, MI: Brazos

that humans are *homo sapiens*, that is, the types of beings that employ wisdom. But what about *homo liturgicus*, that is, are humans the types of beings that worship? This is not merely an observation that humans build temples, churches, and mosques, while squirrels do not. It is an assertion that we instinctively know that there is something more and that we were meant for something more.

We all have a number one in life. It might be our nation-state, family, political party, righteous cause, or job. It might be something a bit shallower like our looks, our social standing, our kid's athletic career, the letters behind our names, or the amount of money in our bank accounts. These are the idols that our pastors and teachers warned us about. Usually, the warning was to not treat these things like gods. Fair enough. But the warning should have been also, "These things *will act* like gods." Think about it. They demand our attention, our time, our talents, sometimes even our treasure. We give offerings to these gods. We give ourselves to these gods. We hold onto them for meaning. We look to them for our identity and value. They even control our lives with a liturgical calendar. There are rituals involved, repeated actions that form our thoughts and actions. There are symbols and artwork, probably some music too. There will be preachers and teachers, sermons, and catechisms. We are the types of beings that worship. We all have a number one and that number one often consumes us.

Part of the problem is that we mix up the ultimate with the penultimate. The ultimate is, by definition, the last and the most important. It is the final destination, the destiny. The penultimate is what comes right before the ultimate either in chronology or importance. Christ claims to be the ultimate, the beginning and the end. He is our destiny (a heavenly end with him), and he is also our ultimate identity (we are righteous in him). This bold claim of Christ (to be our "be all and end all") is not a law preaching; it is a gift preaching. Thus, worship in him is not really about our action toward him as if he were a narcissist demanding that we kiss his ring. Is our God this insecure? No, he demands all of this so that we can have what he always intended to give us, and that is life and love.

Press, 2019), and his three volume Cultural Liturgies Series (Grand Rapids, MI: Baker Academic).

All those other "gods" demand but never give. They cannot do otherwise. And this is our fault. We are asking something from these "gods" that they cannot accomplish. When we ask a nation-state, a political party, or, in some cases, our favorite politician, to be our ultimate identity, we are asking for something they cannot deliver. They cannot be our ultimate destination because they are penultimate. When we make the penultimate ultimate, we are destined for failure. We should make very clear, however, that all these things we make into gods are good. They are gifts to be enjoyed but not gods to be worshipped. We miss out on joy when we ask these things to deliver for us what only God can. Only God can love you back in the unconditional way you need to give you eternal value.

Perhaps there is something deeper. *Homo sapiens* is *homo liturgicus* but also *homo iustificans*.[3] We are the types of beings that seek to be justified, and we are the types of beings that are justified by Christ; that is, Jesus didn't die for the rocks but for us. Nobody wakes up in the morning and desires to be devalued that day. Nobody seeks a meaningless life. Those who have fallen into such melancholy would not wish their predicament on anyone. We seek to be justified. This desire to be justified plays out in our worship. *Homo iustificans* is outwardly *homo liturgicus.* You know where a man seeks his justification by following his worship.[4] Is it on the athletic field or in the boardroom? Is it nation-state, money, prestige, and all the other "gods" mentioned above? Ultimately, he is asking these gods to justify his existence, to make him right (righteous). Or does he give up on the attempt to justify himself and find his justification in Christ?

The truth is that we are always trying to justify ourselves in some way or form. We seek value, importance, and righteousness apart from the gift of Christ. It is, in the end, a righteousness by law and

---

[3] Gregory Schulz, "Nisi Per Verbum: A Disputation Concerning Postmodernism and the Pastoral Office" Logia XXVII:4, 32.

[4] Worship is not only trust because of the theological argument offered above but also because it is how humans think and act in everyday life. When you follow a person's worship (their rituals, the calendar they follow, how their spaces are designed, where they put their money, etc.), you will find what they trust. You will find their god.

not a righteousness by faith. And it is pure tragedy. Freedom awaits. This changes the way, perhaps, we look at ritual, art, calendars, and all the other items we normally attribute to a worship life. Through the lens of a righteousness by law, we see rituals as laws to be fulfilled. We either embrace that (so as to feel righteous) or we rebel against it (in a lame attempt at self-freedom).

James K.A. Smith, who put into eloquent words what so many of us, religious or not, struggled to articulate, challenges us to a liturgical audit.[5] If we take a liturgical audit of ourselves, we might ask questions like this, "Where do I spend most of my free time? Where are my favorite spaces? What are my traditions? Where do I feel the most important or the most spiritual or make the most memories?" The point is that we are people of time and space. We occupy both and that is not going to change. This means that we have a calendar and that we have rituals; we have spaces in which we feel at home and places that exhilarate us. We have bodies, we have culture, we are a part of groups, and we cannot lift ourselves above time. Ritual is simply unavoidable.[6] So let's take a liturgical audit.

Let's start with buildings. Where are your temples in which you spend your most precious time? The soccer fields? Your office? In front of the television? It could be anywhere. A museum or library. A race track or a college football stadium. If you take pains to notice architectural nuances, for example, the lightning or the flow of people in these spaces, you will notice what is important about these spaces and what the high priests of these places want to preach to you. For the ancient buildings of the Christian church, it was often

---

[5] James K.A. Smith, *You Are What You Love*, 126-131.

[6] Congregations have three options when it comes to ritual: Ritual without teaching. This is "going through the motions" and is despised by God because it leads to a false piety, a righteousness by law. The second option is to have teaching without ritual. It sounds nice but is inadequate. Why not have artwork, traditions, and holidays, etc. This helps build the faith and the faith community. The truth is this is also impossible. Even if a congregation took away all art, music, tradition, calendars, and rituals, that minimalism would be a tradition in itself, and that tradition would reflect their theology. The third and best option is both ritual and teaching. We must teach our children why we do the things we do.

to house the grand jewels of Christ's body and blood.[7] These "sermons in stone" centered around the gift of Holy Communion (or the Sacrifice of the Mass depending on your theological bent). Other places you enter preach to you too. Does not the theater press us into a communal experience of entertainment? Do not the acoustics of a stadium move us to a communal, maybe even tribal, passion for one team over another?

Let's consider college football in America for a moment. Think about the colors of sports teams (or tractors companies for that matter). Think of the cheers and the fight songs. Think of the money and time poured into Saturday tailgating or television viewing. Think of the traditions handed down in almost sacred reverence to the next generation.

How about your calendar? You probably have many. If you have schooled-aged kids there will be a September to May school calendar filled with a daily rhythm dotted with recitals, practices, and special holidays unique to school. There is a national holiday schedule (e.g., Halloween to Thanksgiving to Christmas), a sports schedule (e.g., opening day of baseball, Super Bowl Sunday), a seasonal schedule (e.g., spring planting, pumpkins in fall), not to mention your work calendar (e.g., the end of a quarter or fiscal year), and a family schedule "we always take this week off to see his family", and all of them vie for your time. They demand your attention.

Lastly, what are your rituals? Is your routine about fitness the most important ritual in your life? What is your typical routine on Saturday morning like? Sunday morning? How about Saturdays in the fall? The morning coffee, the mixing of a drink, grilling in summer, the shopping on Black Friday. The "ritual" of these events is a major part of the joy, isn't it? Not a bad thing. But ritual habits orient us to what we truly believe is the ultimate.

If you take this liturgical audit seriously and ask yourself what your temples are, your calendars, and your rituals, you will find your gods. Or you will find a balanced life in which the penultimate stays penultimate and the ultimate remains ultimate. In the latter, there is a God who loves you first instead of demanding everything from

---

[7] Justo Gonzalez, *The Story of Christianity* Vol. 2 (Peabody, MA: Prince Press, 1984), 219-221.

you. In the latter, you are set free to actually enjoy the penultimate things precisely because they are not ultimate. You enjoy Christmas because it is about Christ for you instead of manufacturing perfect memories. You enjoy your child's soccer match instead of pacing the pitch with your jaw clenched ready to blow up at the referee or volunteer coach. You enjoy a shopping trip without climbing over other consumers for the last pair of jeans you think will give you some sort of holy (set apart) status. The other gods imprison you. The God of Abraham, Isaac, and Jacob frees you.

What We Miss

It is difficult for post-enlightenment Westerners to appreciate how central physical worship is to being a human. We tend not to think of ourselves as both body and soul. We might even fall into the trap of seeing ourselves as machines. We go to the doctor for an oil change and checkup as if we were automobiles. At best we are "thinking-things" to borrow the famous designation given by René Descartes. Brains on a stick. Our spirituality is quite intellectual. I do not mean that it is necessarily intelligent (often times it is not), but that it is information based. Just give me the facts. No wonder American worship in particular often resembles a university hall lecture or a self-help seminar.[8] We want the information given to us straight. No mystery, no symbolism. We crave practicality. But how often did Jesus speak this way? Rarely. And when he did it was more often than not about the cross, at which his own followers scoffed (see Mark 8:27-38).

This modern mindset has led us to miss some key aspects of Old Testament culture and worship that leads us to a poorer rather than richer view of our own worship. Permit me two examples. First, we struggle to understand coming into the presence of God, and second, we fail to see the importance of what we might call table fellowship.

---

[8] Certainly, there are exceptions such as Pentecostal worship but even this is not about the physical presence of God but rather the Spirit taking over a person's body.

Boundaries in our contemporary world are important, but not for the same reason that boundaries were important in ancient Israel. Today, borders are primarily for protection. They were about protection in Israel too, but in ancient Israel boundaries also marked how close or far away one was from the holiness of God. Yes, God is everywhere, but he chooses to be found in specific places. Can I find God in nature? Sure, but he wants to be found primarily in his Word. Where was God from the time of Moses until incarnation? In the tabernacle and then the temple, specifically in the Holy of Holies on his "throne," the Ark of the Covenant. A pillar of cloud by day and a pillar of fire by night also marked this presence in the early years of Israel's independence from Egypt.

It took a while for Israel to build God a proper home, the Temple, but once settled, boundaries or barriers developed. The Gentile nations were on the other side of the boundary of the Promised Land. In this Holy Land there was a holy city, Jerusalem. On the east end of this holy city there was a holy temple. We are inching closer to God! The temple grounds also had boundaries; there was a Gentile courtyard (the nations), another for the Jewish women and children, another for the men, and another for the priests, in which they made sacrifices. Then there was a building with two rooms. The two rooms were called the Holy Place and the Most Holy Place (the Holy of Holies). The priest on duty could enter the Holy Place, which housed the Bread of Presence on a table, a lampstand endlessly burning oil, and an altar of incense. A curtain separated the Holy Place from the Most Holy Place, one last barrier. In the Holy of Holies resided the Ark of the Covenant. Only the High Priest was permitted to enter this room and only once a year, on the Day of Atonement. There, in the presence of God, who sat on his "throne," the Ark of the Covenant, the High Priest made atonement for the sins of the people.

Most of us can appreciate the symbolism that the curtain, the final barrier, was ripped in two upon Jesus's death, meaning that we have access to God through Christ. No more mediating priests, no more sacrifices, just love and grace. But it is not so much that we don't have to think about the presence of God anymore. He still seeks to be found in certain locations. Nor does the rending of the curtain eliminate the need for a priest. The point is that Jesus is our priest and since he is truly God, we do not have a barrier anymore between us and God. God comes to us.

Perhaps, then, we should ask the question, "Where do we find this Jesus?" or "Who is present?" when we worship. It is still about location. Yes, God is everywhere, but he seeks to be found where he desires to be found, and this is for our benefit. The presence of God is a terribly important issue both in the Scriptures and the Divine Service. Think about the story of the Ten Lepers, the classic Thanksgiving Day text. From the Gospel of Luke:

> Now on his way to Jerusalem, Jesus traveled along the border between Samaria and Galilee. As he was going into a village, ten men who had leprosy met him. They stood at a distance and called out in a loud voice, "Jesus, Master, have pity on us!"
>
> When he saw them, he said, "Go, show yourselves to the priests." And as they went, they were cleansed.
>
> One of them, when he saw he was healed, came back, praising God in a loud voice. He threw himself at Jesus's feet and thanked him—and he was a Samaritan. Jesus asked, "Were not all ten cleansed? Where are the other nine? Was no one found to return and give praise to God except this foreigner?" Then he said to him, "Rise and go; your faith has made you well." (Luke 17:11-19)

I'd wager that many of you have heard basically the same sermon dozens of Thanksgiving mornings. The line of thought goes like this. "Jesus does good things for us, and we should thank him. Where are the other nine this morning? Did not Jesus die for them too? We have so much to be thankful for, so make sure you thank God for everything you have in this great country of ours." You go home thankful and feeling pretty good about yourself too because you were the one who turned to thank your Lord while the other nine were who knows where. "I think I deserve some pie and football," you say to yourself on the car ride home. In a similar way, our worship becomes this shallow. It is paying respect to the one who did good things for us. Almost a polite quid pro quo relationship. Yet there is so much more going on in this text and on our Sunday mornings.

I believe that the point of the Ten Lepers story is not to slam the nine lepers for being ungrateful but rather to ask the question, "Where is God?" A careful look at the text shows that the lepers did exactly what Jesus told them to do. They obeyed him! They went to show themselves to the priests, which was in accordance with Jewish ceremonial cleansing regulations (Leviticus 14). And who is to say that they did not give thanks to God the Father when they went to his house, the Temple? I am sure they were thankful. Who wouldn't be? The problem was that they failed to realize that the true God of Abraham, Isaac, and Jacob actually stood right before them. They failed to realize that the presence of God was on the move, and he happened to be standing right in front of them.

We encounter the living God on Sunday mornings. Or better yet, he encounters us. Do we realize that we are encountering God? This is holy ground. Maybe we are so worried about the intellectual part of worship at times—how we praise, pray, and give thanks or even the rubrics, rituals, and movements—that we miss the obvious: we are standing before God. He comes to preach to us, feed us, wash us, and absolve us. We might be eager to run to the Temple, as is good and right, so to do that we turn our backs on the God who has met us where we are in Word and Meal. If we first start with his saving presence for us, then we rightly praise and thank him. From there we concern ourselves with the grammar of prayer and rubrics of movement not for their own sake but for the sake of the comfort of sinners whom Jesus has encountered.

Similarly, it matters with whom we eat. Breaking bread is not just a physical matter. It is a soul thing. In a fast-paced life, food equals fuel. Eating is like filling up the gas tank of an automobile. Humans as machines again! But for the vast majority of people in the past and even today, eating is spiritual. I do not mean that it is necessarily religious (although it is in many cases) or that the spirit actually consumes the food but rather that dining with another person or other people is more than physical. Perhaps a better way to put it is that eating is a soul thing as much as it is a body thing. Why? Because eating is communal. It is an event. Eating marks important events like weddings or state dinners. Eating and drinking create moments that last in memories. Cultural rituals around eating and drinking connect people across generations. Sharing a table with others connects us on a level deeper than standing in line at a fast-food restaurant. Food is meant to be savored as is the conversation and company around the table. It is as much a soul thing as it is a physical thing. So it matters with whom you break bread.

This is true from the very beginning. Eating in the Garden of Eden was a part of our first parents' worship. It is also part of who we are as humans regardless of religion. If the heads of state of two important but warring countries publicly break bread together, geopolitics are shaken and markets go crazy. We don't invite just anybody over for dinner, let alone to a family wedding. Breaking bread with someone supposes some sort of fellowship or at least the hope of friendship and peace between two individuals, families, or even states. It is an understood part of all human culture. No wonder then that Jesus got in trouble for his dinner companions. Jews were not to eat with Gentiles. That would have assumed a tacit agreement. Add to this the clean/unclean distinction of Jewish law, and Jesus finds himself in hot water with the Pharisees on more than one occasion.

Let's talk a little more about being clean or unclean. The clean/unclean laws of the Old Testament accomplished three tasks. They first kept the Israelites healthy. Secondly, they kept a cultural hedge around Israel. And finally, they catechized the Israelites about sin. The health of the Israelite nation was maintained with quarantine laws regarding skin diseases. This is the first and practical benefit of the clean/unclean distinction. A person with a skin disease needed to be separate from the community. There was also a cultural reason for the clean/unclean distinction. Different dietary restrictions (some foods are clean, some unclean) built a cultural hedge around ancient Israel. It was one way Israel was separate. They survived as a distinct nation and culture when others did not. It actually worked. You can still find Israel on a map but whatever happened to the Hivites? This is all important because God was not only preserving his people but the line of the Savior through his people.

The clean/unclean distinction was also catechetical in nature. The Israelites were taught these lessons: 1. A person cannot help but be unclean. How could a woman stop her menstrual cycle which made a woman unclean? 2. This inevitable uncleanness was often tied to life and death (menstrual cycle, nocturnal emission, giving birth, contact with a corpse). Uncleanness (sin) is handed down throughout the generations and results in death. 3. One must be cleansed from an outside source (the priest). You cannot rid yourself of sin. 4. A person must be clean (holy) before entering the presence of God. Sinners don't go to heaven, only those washed clean in the blood of Christ.

Underneath this all is the concept of transfer. The uncleanness of a corpse or of an unbelieving Gentile could be transferred to an Israelite. It was not in an Israelite's best interest to eat with Gentiles, to touch a corpse, or to eat forbidden and unclean food. Quite frankly, it would have been a nuisance. It would have also broken cultural taboos and would seem to be questioning religious teaching. Fast-forward to Jesus. He was not one to make waves for the sake of making waves. He was not a rebel without a cause. When he broke these cultural taboos and questioned religious teaching (of the leaders of the day, not of Scripture), he was making a theological point. The point is that he was clean (righteous), and he came to deliver this cleanness (righteousness) to the unclean (the sinner).

Perhaps the fullest New Testament example of this is when Jesus approached the town of Nain (Luke 7:11-17). There were two processionals that day, one of death, the other of life. A death had occurred in the town of Nain, the one and only son of a widow. He was all she had. The emotions were raw. The whole town gathered to take their dead outside the city walls before sundown. The emotions were fresh. As the funeral procession approached the town gate, they were met by another parade. Jesus approached the same gate with a parade of followers. Who would go first? The procession of death or the procession of life? All polite societies would answer that the funeral procession has the right of way. But not on that day. Jesus does the rude thing. He goes first. He even does the unthinkable; he touches the bier (the coffin). It would have been an odd scene in any era but especially in that time and place. Didn't Jesus know that the uncleanness of the corpse would be "transferred" to him? Jesus flips the scene upside down. It is not that Jesus becomes unclean but that the dead boy becomes clean. The boy lives! He is no longer unclean (dead) but alive. When Jesus ate with sinners, he was not contracting their disease of sin and uncleanness; he was offering his righteousness to them. He would break bread with anybody because he could save anybody with his perfect life and innocent death.

It is no mere cultural artifact that Christian worship involves eating. It is who we are. It is who God made us to be. It is how we commune with others, and it is how we commune with God. But how could we ever approach a holy God? How could we ever dare to sit at his table? Does sin have fellowship with righteousness? Absolutely not. Still, we are invited. How does this work out? Because God creates what is pleasing to him.[9] We do not earn the invitation. We have no right being at the table. We have no banquet clothes. So, God gives us the banquet clothes of his righteousness. He creates an honored guest. He eats with us because we are clean.

I cannot help but think of Isaiah's angels when thinking about dining with the Lord in Holy Communion. Traditionally, the church sings the angelic song right before Holy Communion, "Holy, holy, holy" (Isaiah 6:3 and Revelation 4:8). It makes sense that we would sing heaven's song when heaven (Christ's body and blood) crashes together with earth. But it is more than this grand wonder that occupies our minds and hearts at this thrilling moment in the Divine Service. We cannot help but say what Isaiah said, "'Woe to me!' [Isaiah] cried. 'I am ruined! For I am a man of unclean lips, and I live among a people of unclean lips, and my eyes have seen the King, the Lord Almighty.'" Isaiah knew he had no business standing before God's fearsome angels who were attending to the heavenly altar. He was rightly petrified. That is when "one of the seraphim flew to [Isaiah] with a live coal in his hand, which he had taken with tongs from the altar. With it he touched [Isaiah's] mouth and said, 'See, this has touched your lips; your guilt is taken away and your sin atoned for'" (Isaiah 6:5-7). Heaven touched Isaiah, and he did not die but rather lived. God enters our space and touches us with words that beat upon ear drums and are written with ink on paper, with water that splashes, with a bit of bread and a sip of wine, and we do not die but live. We are no longer unclean; we are clean. We are no longer sin; we are righteousness (2 Corinthians 5:21). We stand on holy ground in the presence of God, and we stand right with God. He creates what is pleasing to him.

The end of Isaiah, chapter six, which we just discussed, includes the sending of the prophet to speak truth to Israel and, really, the

---

[9] LW 31:57.

whole world. Isaiah's story was not ending; it was only beginning. So it is with New Testament worshippers today. The story of the liturgy goes out into the world. It goes out through Christians as they carry out their vocations and as the ministry of the church speaks truth to their immediate neighbors and the whole world. St. Paul hints at this, perhaps, with the opening lines of chapter twelve of his letter to the Romans when he urges his listeners "to offer your bodies as a living sacrifice, holy and pleasing to God—this is your true and proper worship" (Romans 12:1). Our true worship occurs when we go out into the world to be who God has made us to be, righteous actors of love and speakers of truth. Christians daringly entered the presence of God and survived. By the grace of God, they more than survive, they are loved. Sunday morning is far more about God's action than human action. Sunday is about what God has done for us. It is the story of Christ in poetry and prose. This is what sinners need before they are pushed back out into the world. Sunday is for receiving God's good gifts in faith; the rest of the week is for worship.

The Story of Christ in Poetry and Prose

The following fills in the gaps from the story in part one of this book. Each part of the Divine Service has its own section as before. I make no claim that the following is what the church had in mind when the synagogue worship developed or when Gregory the Great made his reforms or at any other time in history. It is not. Nor do I claim that this is the only way worship should be conducted or has been conducted. It is simply a way to teach about Christ and engage the worshipper with law and gospel.[10]

Bells

The ringing of bells to start the service has no real biblical history. It once served the practical purpose of letting the townspeople and

---

[10] This idea does not originate with me. I am indebted to Rev. David Kind and his little book *About Our Liturgy: Meaning, History and Practice* (Minneapolis: Musolf Press, 2003).

farmers in the field know church will soon begin. Despite the modern conveniences of clocks, the church still uses this robust and beautiful call to worship, perhaps like the trumpeting voice John heard as he entered the worship of heaven (Revelation 1:10). We sit up straight and prepare ourselves for what is to come.

Processional Hymn

The processional hymn is another ancient practice with practical purposes that has become a wonderful tradition in the church. Early Christians, again without wristwatches and alarm clocks, gathered on Sunday morning and awaited the arrival of the town's bishop to begin the Divine Service. Psalms and hymns were sung as people arrived at staggered times. Our opening hymn sets the tone for the Divine Service in general and may have a relation to the theme of that particular Sunday in the year.

A procession may parade up the aisle during the opening hymn. It may include clergy, choirs, acolytes, and even the congregation waving palm branches on Palm Sunday. The procession is led by a crucifer carrying a crucifix and possibly torchbearers carrying torches (candles). This type of procession has its history in the culture of the Mediterranean, specifically the legions of the Roman Army. A gold standard with an eagle atop led the Roman soldiers into battle. The men rallied around the gilded creature much like a modern military may rally around its nation's flag. It seems odd for the church to incorporate a practice with such violent implications, until you see what is on her "standard"—a dying Christ. Isn't that typical of our God? Here we see the theology of the cross in contrast to the theology of glory. It is through the suffering and death of Christ that victory over sin, death, hell, and the devil is gained, not through warfare or political power-plays. The procession into church is dripping with irony. The Root of Jesse stands as "a banner for the peoples; the nations will rally to him" (Isaiah 11:10), but he does not come in glory. Before the service even starts, the faithful are grotesquely focused on their hope and joy—the cross.

Hear St. Paul's words to the Corinthians about the foolishness of God and man's wisdom center on the cross, and not just any cross, but a cross with visible death on it, a crucifix. "We preach Christ crucified," Paul writes (1 Corinthians 1:25). Notice that he did not say, "Crucified and resurrected" even though he did preach both. He makes the point that the crucifixion is "a stumbling block to Jews and foolishness to Gentiles" (1 Corinthians 1:23). It is not wise by our standards. Nobody wants to see a man die such a terrible death. Nobody wants a God that dies. We look at the awful scene anyway because it is our salvation. It is proper to follow the crucifix in (as we would a bride) and to bow the head slightly as it passes, acknowledging what he has done.

Invocation

The invocation calls the Holy Trinity to be with the church. It is a bold move for such a ragtag bunch. The Triune Name that is invoked calls attention to the only reason such a people could be so bold—baptism. It was with the same Triune Name that the faithful were adopted into the family of God. Now we can call upon our Father, and he will listen. The invocation is not a sorcerer mumbling spells to wake a sleeping giant; this is a Father-child relationship. Without those adopting waters, the Almighty remains an over-shadowing presence of doom, but with the sacrament of initiation, we can cry out "Abba, Father," (Romans 8:15) and he listens.

Although the invocation carries our thoughts back to the font, it is not just about our individual relationship with the Father. We have siblings in this grand family. They stand around us in the pews, in other churches around the globe, and around the throne in heaven. Like all families there is tension from time to time, yet the people we worship with are our brothers and sisters. We may not always like them all the time; we may have never become friends with them, if it weren't for church, but they are still our family. Kind of like our biological families! In fact, the spiritual family of the Father gathers in a very similar way to every biological family no matter what the culture. A person would be hard pressed to find a family reunion that did not involve these three elements and perhaps nothing more: eating, drinking, and conversing. That's what families do. The family of Father, Son, and Holy Spirit gathers together on Sundays for the same. We talk about our family, our faults, our future, and our perfect Father and Brother, and then we eat and drink.

A wonderful practice that unites the invocation with a baptismal remembrance is the sign of the cross. It reminds us of Christ's saving death and our intimate connection to that death in baptism (Romans 6:3-6). Most were "marked as one redeemed by Christ crucified" at baptism. The sign of the cross placed upon the child (or adult) is a symbol of his or her death into Christ. It marks us as belonging to God. This action is reminiscent of God's instructions to Aaron and the priests on how to bless Israel. "So they will put my name on the Israelites, and I will bless them" (Numbers 6:27).

The sign of the cross can be employed from that special day as a reminder of baptism. It is such a wonderful physical reminder that Luther recommends it at least twice daily.[11] Despite its abuses, the sign of the cross remains a valuable devotional tool for the faithful. What a comfort it is to wake up in the morning, make the sign of the cross and say, "Give me your best, world! You can take my money, my house, my car; you can even take my freedom and my life. I've already died. I belong to God forever. Nothing can touch me!" It puts the rest of the day's failures and triumphs into an eternal perspective.

Versicles

It is true that we are able to approach our God without fear of condemnation. A parent's love is the strongest of loves. Add divine perfection to it, and that love is unbreakable. Still, we do not come without fear. After all, "the fear of the Lord is the beginning of wisdom" (Psalm 111:10). There is a healthy dose of fear in a good father-child relationship. We approach our Father with a little trepidation and that is for good reason—our sin. The versicles are short sentences, usually from the psalms, that give the faithful a sense of holy awe as they "go to the altar of God" (Psalm 43:4).

Confession

No matter the station in life, the first thing a person says in the presence of such potential wrath is, "I'm sorry." The king and the peasant say the same thing because the Almighty and his demanding law dwarf all. Confession and absolution are just as personal an encounter with

---

[11] SC VII, 1, 4.

God as was Christ's meeting with the woman by the well (John 4:1-26). All that burden is unloaded and stricken from the record book with the divine words, "I forgive." The confession and absolution are technically not a part of the Divine Service. Holy Absolution is a stand-alone rite. The lack of participation in private absolution has forced the church to place absolution into the corporate life of the church. It is the hope of all that the opportunity to confess and be absolved privately be more readily available and taken advantage of in the future. Until then, we confess and are forgiven together.

A moment of silence before the confession (or *Confiteor*) may be observed to recall the total depravity of mankind. If one has trouble coming up with specific sins committed, Luther's words may help, "Consider your place in life according to the Ten Commandments. Are you a father, mother, son, daughter, employer, employee? Have you been disobedient, unfaithful, or lazy?"[12] As we will see at the end of the Sunday morning journey, our vocations in life lift humanity to a "startling degree,"[13] but at this point our performance brings us shame. We throw ourselves at the mercy of the court (Luke 18:13), especially considering that we do not confess only the sins we cognizantly commit, but also our sinful nature. We admit both our actual and original sin.

Often, the faithful will kneel for prayers, psalms, the *Kyrie*, and the confession of sins. Kneeling adds a third posture to the worship of the church along with standing and sitting. Each is unique. We stand to confess our faith with creeds and song, we kneel to pray and confess our sins, and we sit to receive by listening. This physical repentance of kneeling has a long history in the Scriptures from Abraham before his heavenly visitors (Genesis 18:2) to the descriptions of the end times (Philippians 2:10, Romans 14:11).

Absolution

Nothing transpires between the confession and the absolution. Don't let this absence pass unnoticed. This void is what makes Christianity

---

[12] SC V, 20

[13] Gene Edward Veith Jr., *The Spirituality of the Cross* (St. Louis: Concordia Publishing House, 1999), 72.

different from anything else, religious, or not. It gives Christians a reason to smile in the face of so much heartache. It allows peace in the middle of chaos. It allows hope to exist. In this astonishing absence we find true love. We owe God everything, but he takes nothing. The greatest gift we can receive, eternal life, is given for free. No money exchanges hands, no work is needed, no payment necessary. We come as the prodigal children, and even before we can offer our plan to make up for our misdeeds, our Father has the fattened calf slaughtered (Luke 15:11-32). Nothing comes between the confession and the absolution (2 Samuel 12:13). Nothing. What a relief this is.

Another subtlety worth our attention is the exact wording of the absolution. It may seem like a small matter that the pastor says, "I forgive" instead of "God forgives." "It's just a matter of semantics," as the dismissive phrase goes. That is until we try to console a murderer by abortion or an adulterer by prostitution, whose guilt is so great they doubt forgiveness given with this degree of separation (that is "God forgives" instead of "I forgive"). It is true that only the Divine may forgive, but God's incarnational and sacramental ways bring forgiveness directly to us. Jesus Christ couldn't have made it any clearer, "If you forgive anyone his sins, they are forgiven; if you do not forgive them, they are not forgiven" (John 20:23).

Christ's words to his apostles are reason enough to heed the warning of the Lutheran Confessors, "It would be unconscionable to remove private absolution from the church. Moreover, those who despise private absolution know neither the forgiveness of sins nor the power of the keys."[14] It is very easy for a troubled soul to say, "If pastor knew what I did last night, he would not forgive me." It is harder to doubt when the pastor hears the sin privately and still says, "I forgive." Private absolution isn't only Roman Catholic; it is Christian.

Introit

We have reached the actual beginning of the Divine Service. The introit is nothing more than an entrance, which is what the word "introit" means. The introit evolved much like the processional

---

[14] Ap. XII, 100-101.

hymn. In many congregations it is still the cover music for the procession. Songs were naturally sung before and as the service began. Psalm verses were chosen to fit the theme of each day of the church year. A comprehensive schedule of psalms developed for the entire church year. Notice the importance of entering the presence of God with both the processional and now the introit.

Kyrie Eleison

Now that we are officially in the presence of our God, we beg, "Have mercy on us." We do not come to worship in order to show off our abilities, works, or even to praise God, but rather to receive mercy. The parable of the Pharisee and the tax collector shows us the way to properly approach our God (Luke 18:9-14). The *Kyrie Eleison* (Lord, have mercy) is a little different than the "I'm sorry" of the confession spoken moments before. This is a cry for mercy in all aspects of our life. As the *Kyrie* is sung there is a sense of the greater sins of humanity. The *Kyrie* is about more than the individual faults of an individual soul. This is a cry for deliverance from all the results of sin: natural disasters, diseases, starvation, tyrants, terrorists, and demons.

Although thoroughly biblical, the origins of this song are found in the Roman Empire. When a ruler entered a village, his subjects would naturally beg something along these lines, "Lord (or sir) have mercy!" We utter the same as we come into the presence of our King. Not only do we depend on him for everything, but he has the power and the right to punish us. We can't give to him, but he can give to us, so we beg, "Mercy!"

Once again, we come across some delicious irony. Our Lord Jesus Christ was called "lord" just as any person of importance was in that time period. However, the word had an even deeper meaning for the Jews. Four letters in Old Testament Hebrew (יהוה) made up the name of the true and only God of Abraham, Isaac, and Jacob. So holy was this name that generations of Israelites would not dare say it out loud. When one read the Scriptures, the word "Lord" was uttered in place of the holy Name of God. It was a big deal for a carpenter's son from Nazareth to be called "*Kyrios*" or "Lord" (Luke 6:5 and Matthew 14:30). They were calling him God! As we approach our God, our Lord, our *Kyrios*, we say, "Have mercy!" because he is the only one who can protect us.

Gloria in Excelsis

God the Father answered ancient Israel's prayer for mercy the same way he answers our prayer for mercy, with the Messiah. He is the one Israel longed for, and he is the one we need. He is not necessarily what we wanted (Jesus wasn't what many in Israel wanted), and he certainly isn't what we expected. Instead of bags of money falling from the sky, the cure for cancer discovered the day after a diagnosis, or perfect children who fulfill all our expectations, God gives us a babe placed in the feeding trough of animals.

The *Gloria in Excelsis* (Glory in the highest) is a song of praise sung to the Father in heaven for his mercy and forgiveness. It is sometimes replaced with another song of praise. It is truly fitting, however, to sing the song of the angelic host at this moment in the Divine Service. Ancient Israel cried out for mercy from their razed towns and constant funerals. The Lord answered their cry with the Messiah. In the same way, we prodigal children cry with audible pain in our voices, "Mercy!" and our Father answers, "Jesus Christ." It makes sense to respond as the heavens did that night outside Bethlehem, "Glory to God in the highest!" (Luke 2:14). Our prayers for mercy have been answered. Notice the change in music from the *Kyrie* to the *Gloria*. The law makes the *Kyrie* dour; the gospel makes the *Gloria* joyful.

The Divine Service wasn't planned out by a committee centuries ago with the ingenious idea of retelling the story of Christ through song and poetry. Rather, it developed to include the major parts of Christ's life. What else would we sing about? With the Christmas song of the angels, we begin our journey through Christ's life. As any good biographer does, the Divine Service foreshadows the greatness of the man whose story it tells. The *Gloria* also gives us a glimpse into the future. The audience is told right away why this man is so important that a whole hour will be spent telling his story. Of course, he is more than a man of history. We have a vested interest in all of this. His life becomes our life. If he fails at this or that test of perfection, if he falls to his knees before Satan in the desert (Matthew 4:9-10), if he succumbs to temptation and spits right back at the crowd (Mark 14:65), if he does not rise again (Luke 24:5-8), if he is a fraud, then we have nothing. Then he does not become our sin, and we do not become his righteousness (1 Corinthians 5:21). Then the whole world is lost.

We need to see the cute babe of Bethlehem live a perfect life in our place. We need to see the Virgin's baby boy pay the perfect price for my depravity. We need to see beyond the small town of Bethlehem northeast to the sloping hills of Zion. We need to see him on the cross. So, we sing the angels' ode (Luke 2:14) and John's dirge (John 1:29) all at once. We are told that the cute babe of Bethlehem will be led to the slaughter like a lamb.

Salutation

All of the above has been a prelude of sorts. There has been some pomp and circumstance as we enter the presence of God, but it is "lowly pomp" as the Palm Sunday hymn writer calls it.[15] "I'm sorrys" and cries for mercy have been uttered. Direct forgiveness and a brief synopsis of the salvation story have come from a merciful God. Now the Service is ready to start. A greeting is in order and not the happy "hellos" and the standard "good mornings" offered in the narthex. This is something different; mere pleasantries will not do. A more formal and spiritual "The Lord be with you" followed by the response "And with your spirit" (or "And also with you") are given back and forth. We use this common greeting many faithful Israelites employed in the past (Ruth 2:4, Luke 1:28).

The salutation can reflect the understanding of ordination. It is obvious to all, with a few exceptions of some strapping young reverends, that the man up front on Sunday is no better than the rest of the congregation—and that's putting it politely (2 Corinthians 4:7). Again, we see the ingenious way God operates. The office of pastor is not about the talents of one man. It is about the power of the gospel. The Lord made Gideon fight with 300 men against the combined armies of the "eastern peoples" so that no one could boast. When victory came, everybody knew from where the power came (Judges 7). Everybody knows where the talent lies when hundreds show up for

---

[15] LSB 441:2

Easter Sunday, and it isn't in the preacher (1 Corinthians 1:21). The focus is on the right place.

The pastor stands in the stead of Christ. He says, "I forgive." He wears a robe to cover himself. This is not about him. It is about Christ and his flock. With the salutation we say, "This is the guy. He has a divine call to be here. He is the one who will speak forgiveness, wash sinful babes, and feed the helpless. He is from God, and he has a message of peace. Beautiful are his feet (Isaiah 52:7), even if his belly sticks out and his hairline is receding. Blessed is he because he is here to speak forgiveness!"

Prayer of the Day

Christians start occasions with prayer. It is one of the benefits of baptism. We can say, "Abba, Father," because he is our Father. We have the full rights of sonship (Romans 8:15). So, it is natural that Sunday morning begins with a prayer. The Prayer of the Day is a terse prayer that focuses our attention on the matter at hand. There is a different prayer for each Sunday describing the theme of that particular day in the church year.

It is good to keep our hands occupied and our eyes closed during prayer to help us focus. Sometimes a pastor's hands may be held out, both exposing the thoughts of the faithful to God and the anticipation of receiving from him. His hands may be raised above his head during the Lord's Prayer indicating that this is the perfect prayer first uttered from Christ's perfect lips.

Readings, Psalms, and Verse of the Day

With the mood set and the greetings out of the way, it is time to get to the business at hand. We are here to hear. The Readings are an extraordinary event as they were in the synagogues our Savior frequented. Those readings came from the Torah, the Prophets, and Writings interspersed with psalms. So it goes today. Usually, an Old Testament reading comes first (or a reading from Acts in the Easter season), followed by a psalm (sometimes referred to as a gradual). A reading from the New Testament comes next followed by the Verse of the Day and the Alleluia. Finally, the Gospel comes as the culmination of the Readings since it is the very words and actions of the incarnate Lord.

The Readings are an extraordinary event because this is our living Lord being presented to us. It is the living voice of Christ. It is not a magical spell, but neither is it a university hall lecture. When he is preached, he is present. These are sacred words. "Do not come any closer," God said to Moses from the burning bush. "Take off your sandals, for the place where you are standing is holy ground" (Exodus 3:5). We might not take off our shoes, but we come in holy awe—God is here. These words have power (Isaiah 55:11). Think of what Jesus witnessed when the seventy-two returned from preaching, "I saw Satan fall like lightning from heaven" (Luke 10:18). Alleluia, indeed!

The Readings are meant to flow together. They often intertwine to serve the theme of the day, which is usually based upon the Gospel selection. Listening carefully to all three readings (and the Psalm, Verse of the Day, and Hymn of the Day) will often give you insights into the Gospel Reading more often than not. Preachers will even incorporate the whole "Word section" into their homilies. Some pericopes (a series of readings) will incorporate a *lectio continua* (a series of readings through a particular book such as Romans) that do not match up with the other selections but even then, there is more often than not a theme that easily runs through all of the Readings.

Alleluia

The word "alleluia" means "Praise you, the Lord." It is another angelic song squeaked out by the church militant. It serves as a musical interlude between the Second and Gospel Readings. It is often sung with the Verse of the Day, which repeats the theme of the day. The Alleluia also serves another purpose. It ratchets things up a notch as we proceed to the Gospel Reading. We have heard the desperate straits of ancient Israel left only with shadows of things to come (Hebrews 10:1). We have heard the doctrinal applications of the apostles with their advantage of hindsight. Now it is time for us to see the real thing, the model that posed for various artists' passionate renderings, the giant whose shadow covered the first centuries of creation. It's time for the Gospels to have their say.

The *Gloria in Excelsis* are often not sung in the more somber or preparatory seasons of Lent and Advent, and the Alleluia is also omitted in Lent. After these seasons, which are characterized by deep repentance, these songs are brought back with much joy on Christmas and Easter. A "Farewell to Alleluia" processional may occur on the last Sunday of Epiphany in preparation for Lent. A banner with the word "Alleluia" on it may exit church at the end of that service. Typically, that Sunday is Transfiguration Sunday. Transfiguration is the perfect transition between the revealed glory of Jesus Christ (Epiphany means manifesting or unveiling) to the repentant preparation of Lent. Peter wanted the glory of the Transfiguration to stay on earth, but Jesus said, "No, we must head to Jerusalem" (see Luke 9:33, 51). We go too.

Gospel Reading, Acclamations, and Processional

No utterance of Holy Writ is useless or unimportant. When the Holy Spirit breathes, we rightfully clamor for understanding. Yet, we understand that it is all about Christ (John 5:39). So the very words and actions of the God-man, that is the Gospel of Jesus Christ according to Matthew, Mark, Luke, or John, are the climax of these Readings. We sing acclamations ("Glory be to God, O Lord!" and "Praise be to you, O Christ!"). We stand and sometimes we even have a processional, in order to say physically and boldly, "This is what we have been waiting for—Christ."

He is the center of the Scriptures and the center of our lives. Without him we have nothing. If we lose him, we lose more than a friend, a teacher, a guidance counselor, a mentor, our inspiration, or whatever else he is to us, or perhaps more accurately, what we make him to be. We lose our life ... forever. In his gracious way, he comes into our lives to be the center. He did it in Bethlehem, and now he does it with Word and Sacrament. It makes beautiful sense to have a processional into the gathered laity with the Gospel Book. During festivals the Gospel Book is carried into the midst of the people and read. This is especially fitting on Christmas Day when the Gospel Reading is from John, "The Word became flesh and made his dwelling among us" (John 1:14). This is how he makes his dwelling among us now—with his Word.

Hymn of the Day

The Hymn of the Day follows the Readings. Before we receive a theologian's commentary on these Readings, we get a poet's perspective. Those who use words as their paint are artists of the first degree. We are privileged to be the recipients of thousands of years of art, often without paying a penny for it. Every people and language are represented as we open up our books of song. Again, we marvel at the way God hones so many different talents to serve one purpose—the clear presentation of grace. With these varied perspectives we see things analytical minds can miss. Who of us would have thought about the Nativity this way, "The Father's love begotten"?[16] How many could pen words as beautiful as "Awake my heart with gladness! See what today has done; now after gloom and sadness, comes forth the glorious sun"?[17] Only a poet could describe the cross like this, "None in foliage, none in blossom, none in fruit thine equal be, symbol of the world's redemption."[18] We are truly blessed to feel the real law and gospel experiences of such poets. No other media but poetry and music can reflect the passion and drama of these salvific events. No wonder J.S. Bach is called the "Fifth Evangelist."

Sermon

The words of the Greek men in the temple cannot be recalled often enough (John 12:21). They wanted Jesus. They needed Jesus, and so do we. The man in the robe has a divine call; he is not a hired man. Congregational oustings have no part in the church and often backfire. At the same time, there is no excuse for laziness or incompetence, which are the cause of too much grief. The laity has a right, no, a duty to demand doctrinal integrity and Christo-centric preaching from its pulpits. The church must demand to see Jesus. It is her right. It is her duty.

Itching ears will lead people to complain about the preacher, and the lure of popularity will tug on that same preacher, but he must put himself away and preach Christ. There are too many important

---

[16] LSB 384:1
[17] LSB 467:1
[18] LSB 454:4

matters to talk about, and there is too much at stake to do anything less. Social gospel, prosperity gospel, eco-gospel, liberation gospel, and all the other pseudo-gospels out there can contain fabulous causes that should be taken up and even led by Christians, but they are not gospel. They are not Christ. If all the preacher accomplishes is making life a little less painful, successes a little more frequent, the world a little cleaner, or society a little more compassionate, but fails to place the hearer into the heavenly realms through Christ and Christ alone, all he has done is make the path to hell a little smoother. "Sir, we would like to see Jesus," is the church's cry because this is the only way we know God. As the axiom states, "Know Christ, know God. No Christ, no God."

The sermon is not didactic although it teaches. It is not an inspiring story although it lifts us up to new heights. It is not a moralistic tale although it leads to a new life. It is not a self-help talk although it guides us. It is not fire and brimstone although it calls sin for what it is. At its basic best, the sermon is an extension of confession and absolution. It makes us shamefully aware of our sins and comforts us with forgiveness. It shakes things up because it brings Christ into our lives.

Notice that the sermon is only one part of the Divine Service. It is not the crescendo of Sunday morning. There is a lot more going on than just the sermon. Every bit of the Service is God's Word. Some of it is a paraphrase, but much of it is taken from Scripture verbatim. It is a mistake to put everything on the shoulders of one man, although he speaks with the Holy Spirit's power. The talent of the preacher does not make a church worthy or unworthy of attendance. The sermon simply guides the listeners back to Scripture and ushers them to the Lord's table.

Creed

An "amen" is collectively spoken after the Word is read and preached. The word "amen" means "true." It is similar to signing your name to a letter agreeing with its content. The creed, which comes from the Latin word for "I believe" (*credo*), is a collective statement of faith. It serves as an "amen" to the Word section of the Divine Service. The church catholic (a word that means universal) uses three ecumenical creeds.

Despite all the divisions in Christendom, necessary and unnecessary, these three creeds are agreed upon: the Apostle's (the baptismal and catechetical creed), the Nicene (used on most Sundays), and the Athanasian (the longest of the three and usually confessed on Trinity Sunday and in some places Christmas Day). Although they each have their own particular histories and their usages, all three are stained with the blood of martyrs.

These creeds did not come out of nowhere but were hammered out because of the great Christological controversies of the early church. To put it simply, some said that Jesus was not completely man; some said that Jesus was not completely God, and the defenders of faith stood up for the truth. They precisely confessed the truth as the Bible teaches. The church is concerned with accurately identifying Christ because he is at the heart of the gospel. If Christ is not completely true man, then he was not truly tempted, and his perfect life and sacrifice are a fraud. If Christ is not completely true God, then he does not have the power to save us. If he is not the God-man, then our salvation is not real.

So that we never forget their battles and so that we never fall into those errors again, we recite their confession every Sunday. Creeds were formed because false doctrine infects the church. Only in a perfect world is there no need for confessions. Since we live in a broken world, we live among heresy both inside and outside the church. Therefore, we must confess. In fact, we are called by our Savior to do so (Matthew 16:15).

I cannot help but compare the creeds to the Pledge of Allegiance. In the United States we pledge allegiance to the flag. Most of us did it every day in elementary school. Regardless of one's politics, most would agree that brave men and women have given their lives for the cause of freedom, as imperfect as it may be this side of heaven. The flag helps us remember that our freedom is not free. We stand and remember. We are grateful. When we confess the creeds, we stand and remember. We also stand to be counted. We understand that there were battles in the past. Brave men and women fought for our freedom. Not political freedom this time but freedom from the snare of false doctrine. And yes, blood was shed. A lot of it. So we stand and remember. So we stand to be counted. We will not fall into the same traps of the Christological or Trinitarian heresies of the past. Why? Because we recite these creeds again and again. We will not forget.

Offertory and Offering

The offering "processional," which some churches include, originally involved bread and wine, with the laity providing the elements for Holy Communion. You can imagine how the problems in Corinth ensued as the rich became drunk and the poor went hungry. The rich brought more than enough but did not share with the less fortunate during these extended agape meals (1 Corinthians 11:17-22).

The offering that was once food-related is now monetary. Of course, our offerings to God are not limited to such a simplified thing as money. The gift of giving is only one of many gifts presented by the Spirit (1 Corinthians 12). Our voices, our instrumental playing, our carpentry, our masonry, our painting, our candle making, our sewing, our polishing, our cleaning, and all the rest are visible in the church. Not to mention the gifts of sharing, consoling, encouraging, and visiting that are exercised outside the church building.

If we haven't already noticed, our gifts to God aren't really for him. He doesn't need our good works in heaven. He has plenty.[19] Our gifts are for our neighbors. As we serve our neighbors, we blindly serve Christ. Jesus will say, to our astonishment, on the Last Day, "I tell you the truth, whatever you did for one of the least of these brothers of mine, you did for me" (Matthew 25:40). Even our praises directed to him are not meant only for him but are meant for the person sitting next to us, the man on the street that cannot help but overhear the noise echoing inside, the connoisseur of music who knows Bach's cantatas, the Christmas shopper who knows the words to "Joy to the World" by heart.

Even in our monetary sacrifices God still makes it about us. Only for the thoroughly self-righteous are offerings a source of pride or a bestowal of power. For most people, their mere pennies are just that, mere pennies. Yet, God uses stewardship to teach a big lesson. We give our first fruits knowing that our jobs could be lost in an instant, we could go on disability in a moment, or our stocks could

---

[19] Wingren, 10.

crash within a day. Despite the risk, God says, "Do not fret, I will pull you through. And remember no matter what happens, I give you heaven because I have given up *my* first fruits, my one and only Son" (see 1 Corinthians 15:23).

Prayer of the Church

We have come to the end of the first part of the Divine Service, the Word section. Soon we will enter the Meal portion. Before the transition, we offer our prayers with those small offerings given moments before. The Prayer of the Church or the General Prayer is just that, a general prayer from the church. While it reflects aspects of the theme of the day, its primary goal is to collect all the worries, requests, petitions, troubles, and uncertainties of the body of Christ.

Like the offerings, God again makes this about us. We are taught the words of love as we are taught to pray. A good father encourages his child to ask for things; he teaches her to say, "I love you," and along the way she learns who provides her protection and her preserves—her parents. Now she knows to whom to go when in need. So it is with our Father. He teaches us where our life comes from, where to go when we are hurt, where to turn when we are in need. Like all caring fathers, he is also good at using the word "no." But still we come, and rightfully so, with all our petitions and requests, knowing that nothing is impossible with God (Matthew 19:26). "You promised you'd take care of me!" we cry with trembling desperation yet strangely confident in the outcome.

Prefaces

We now move to the Meal portion of this family reunion. It is a new section, and so we begin with another salutation. In the early years of the church, the Word and Meal portions of the Divine Service were divided so the catechumens (those adults who were studying and had not yet been baptized and confirmed, as we would call it) could be dismissed. They could not even see the "mysteries" that were to come. Only after much study and a lifestyle change from their pagan ways, were new Christians allowed to approach the table. So, they were dismissed, and the doors were shut. Hence the term "closed communion."

The second preface is quite profound. We are told to "Lift up our hearts" and lift them up we will. There is a passionate joy that comes when we realize that the heavenly creature named Christ is coming to visit, that the same body which hung on the cross for our salvation, which the same blood that poured from his pierced side is now ours. This is a foretaste of the heavenly feast to come. With the lyrics, "We will lift them up to the Lord," we say, "We will dine with my Lord, sing with the angels and commune with our holy family. You better believe that our hearts are lifted high. We will lift them up to the Lord! We have been 'raised with Christ,' so we will 'set our hearts on things above'" (Colossians 3:1).

This ancient meal has many names: "Holy Communion," "The Lord's Supper," "The Sacrament of the Altar." It is also referred to as "The *Eucharist*," the Greek word for thanksgiving. When Jesus ate with his disciples in the upper room, the first Holy Communion, he was eating the Passover meal. As was the custom, a long prayer of thanksgiving and a recounting of God's wonders were included in the meal celebration. You know the words well, "The Lord Jesus, on the night he was betrayed, took bread, and when he had given thanks, he broke it and said…" (1 Corinthians 11:23-24). It is good and right that we should at all times and in all places give thanks to God for all that he has done, from the creation of the world to the day he takes us to paradise. It is truly good and right.

Sanctus and Benedictus

"Therefore, with all the saints on earth and hosts of heaven, we praise [his] holy name and join their glorious song." It is heaven on earth—at least for a brief moment. It is not perfect, but those ancient catechumens left outside were not disappointed when they were finally able to sing with the angels, "Holy, holy, holy!" (Isaiah 6:3, Revelation 4:8). The line between this world and the next is perhaps at its thinnest during the Divine Service. We have lifted up our hearts and eyes, and God has lifted our souls to new heights. Heaven and earth crash together in the Supper.

The story of Christ continues with the song known as the *Sanctus* and *Benedictus* (Holy and Blessed). We find ourselves on Palm Sunday, singing the song of the Jerusalem crowds, "Hosanna,

hosanna, hosanna in the highest. Blessed is he, blessed is he who comes in the name of the Lord."

It is too bad we only have palm branches once a year! They would be waving uncontrollably every Sunday if possible. We understand the enormity of the situation, and we also understand the irony. Here comes our Lord riding so lowly on a donkey; here comes our Lord, in, with, and under the bread and wine. He stoops this low for us. It is no less exciting and no less marvelous on any given Sunday than it was on that Sunday of Holy Week. Here comes our Lord in lowly pomp.

Eucharistic Prayer

As quickly as we were transported to the hill called Zion on Sunday, we are taken to the upper room a few days later on Thursday of Holy Week. The Jewish capital was bustling with excitement during this Holy Week, and it wasn't only because its King made his entrance or that he created such a scene in the temple. It was because it was Passover time. This was a huge deal. Jews from all over the world came to Jerusalem to celebrate the Lord's greatest act of mercy so far. The Lord never let them forget, "I am the Lord your God, who brought you up out of Egypt" (Psalm 81:10). The prophets proclaimed it, the psalmists sang it, and, of course, they stopped everything once a year for this celebratory meal.

This was a meal of remembrance. The story of the Exodus from Egypt was retold, reenacted in a way. Wine, unleavened bread, bitter herbs, and lamb were all served with the proper symbolic meaning attached. The bitter herbs pointed to the bitter slavery of their people. The unleavened bread reminded the Israelites of their hasty exit from Egypt in the middle of the night. Cups of wine were accompanied with blessings. The meal's most important course was the lamb. It was the blood of perfect lambs that saved the Israelite firstborns in Egypt. The angel of the Lord passed over the bloody doorframes of Israel. It was a meal of remembrance—so they would never forget!

It was also a meal of the future. The ultimate goal of the Exodus was the Promised Land, which flowed with milk and honey. A heavenly Promised Land was also waiting. The blood of those lambs saved them from their enemy, the Pharaoh. The blood of the true Lamb of God would save them from their eternal enemies of Satan, sin, hell, and death. The wrath of God passes over those cleansed with the blood of the Lamb. Their journey was bitter at times, but at the end was a fantastic feast with plenty of good wine. Not only did this nostalgic meal point back to the Exodus, it also pointed ahead to the Messiah and his heavenly kingdom.

So Jesus, on the night he was betrayed, reclined with his closest followers to both remember the past and to peer into the future. It would be the last year of looking ahead. This was the year the Lamb of God's blood would finally flow. No longer was this a meal that only looked back to the Exodus and forward to the Messiah. Now it was a meal that looks back to Christ's passion, gives the Messiah, and looks forward to the heavenly feast prepared in the Promised Land of heaven. It all changed when Jesus said, "This is my body" (1 Corinthians 11:24).

As we prepare to approach the table whose guests include Christ, we remember with prayers what God has done. We recline at the table and see "why this night is different from all other nights." The Eucharistic Prayer (or Prayer of Thanksgiving) is similar to the prayers of the Passover meal as it highlights God's grace throughout the years. In the Christian liturgy it holds up the jewel of the *Verba* (or Words of Institution) as the treasure they are.

The Eucharistic Prayer, like many parts of the liturgy, has been corrupted in the past and is therefore omitted from many orders of service. Some claimed that Christ was re-sacrificed in an unbloody manner at Holy Communion, ultimately rooting the gospel right out of the Supper. Man becomes partly responsible for his own salvation if he must participate in some manner with a second sacrifice of Christ. But Christ died once for all (Hebrews 7:24-27). At its evangelical best, the prayer around the *Verba* (there are always some prayers with or without the Eucharistic Prayer) points to the pure grace of God throughout history and the pure grace of the Supper. At its liturgical best, the prayer holds up the Words of Institution as the jewels they are while continuing the story of Christ by inviting the listeners to the upper room.

Verba

These *Verba* are the words that Jesus spoke on that Maundy Thursday night (1 Corinthians 11:23-24). They serve as consecratory words for our meal today. The power of this forgiving meal does not come from mere bread and wine but from the eternal Word. As the Gospel Reading was the climax of the Service of the Word so the *Verba* serve as the climax of the Service of the Sacrament. And important *verba* they are! Much blood has been spilled over these words. Never take for granted how clearly these words are spoken, "This *is* my body." It is not "Jesus *says*, 'This is my body'" as others have proclaimed in order to deny the real presence. There is no silly semantic parsing here. He said what he meant, and he meant what he said. This is his covenant with us, his last will and testament so to speak. He speaks this technical legal language. These words are clear, and we treat them with respect.

He gives us himself in the Sacrament of the Altar. He leaves us with salvation, strengthening of faith, forgiveness, and eternal life. It's better than any rich uncle's will! We proclaim his last will and testament to all as we join him in this heavenly feast (1 Cointhians 11:26).

The Our Father

Following his "Last Supper" (he would have more as we find out later), Christ and some of his closest companions walked out to the Garden of Gethsemane. There he prayed so hard that drops of sweat as thick as blood fell heavily to the ground, pregnant with the burdens of the world. He was burdened with so much weight that he could barely handle it. The guilt of the world, the sin of mankind, the nastiness of humanity were on his shoulders, on his one pair of shoulders. He prayed for his disciples, for the world, and even for himself, "Father, if you are willing, take this cup from me" (Luke 22:42). From this mine full of pressure came a brilliant gem that we can barely utter, if we think about it thoroughly, "May your will be done" (Matthew 26:42).

It is fitting that after we leave the Maundy Thursday table, we move with our Lord into the darkness of Olivet. Even though we are sleepy like Peter, James, and John, even though thoughts of grandeur fill our minds as we unsheathe our swords in the name of the Lord

(Matthew 26:50-52), even though we are evasive in times that call for confession as Peter was later that night (Matthew 26:69-75), we still utter those unthinkable words, "Thy will be done." It is a bold statement we make, especially considering that Jesus made the same statement on the way to his own execution. It is one of many bold confessions we make with nothing of our own to back them up, no real courage, no real machismo, only Christ. We say them despite our own weakness. We say them with Christ as our guarantee. So is the language of faith, "Thy will be done" even if it means our will is not done.

Pax Domini

What happens next may seem strange to us. The pastor turns to face the congregation with host and chalice and says, "The peace of the Lord be with you always," as he traces the sign of the cross. The *Pax Domini* (Peace of the Lord) reminds us of the angelic chorus with which we sang at the beginning of the Service. The peace we proclaimed is not like the Treaty of Versailles or the tranquility of a pacific lake guarded by tall pines. It is the Prince of Peace, who does not bring temporal peace (Matthew 10:35) but real peace. It is true peace because it is for eternity. Although it is for heaven, some of it seeps into our lives right now. The pastor shows us how this Prince of Peace gives us peace, through his body and blood. It is another absolution given before we dine together.

This was the time, during the early years of the Christian church, when the kiss of peace was exchanged between parishioners. Peace with God means that we can have or at least try to have peace with others. In fact, if you are stubbornly unforgiving, then the table of Christ is no place for you. The unrepentant are excluded (1 Corinthians 11:28-29). The sadness of Christian division makes the ancient practice seem quaint. Certainly, the sober-minded Christian of every era knew that divisions would always haunt the body of Christ, but I doubt anyone of them could imagine how many denominations and splinter groups there are today. Peace within the church will always be an allusive thing this side of heaven. Yet in this meal, peace is obtained. Closed communion does remain. The practice of protecting the table is a necessary evil in a sinful world where heretical wolves prowl in sheep's clothing. It is sad, but it is a must. In the meal, however, the unbreakable body of Christ communes with her Lord. We just can't enjoy the benefits of such a perfect fellowship yet. But what were we expecting in a sinful world? The Peace of the Lord will still be with us always.

The imagery of the cup is significant also. When someone wanted to assassinate an important person in the ancient world, poison was a popular choice. The idea of a chalice full of poison would have been familiar. In Gethsemane Jesus spoke of a cup of wrath, full of the poisonous punishment our sins deserved. He asked that the cup be taken away. The answer was "No." So here is he at our tables, giving us a cup of life. He drank the cup of wrath to the dregs and replaced it with his life-giving blood. Now it is a chalice of life.

Agnus Dei

It is now Good Friday in the Divine Service, so to speak. The light of day chases away the darkness of Gethsemane and the High Priest's courtyard. No longer is the ugliness hidden by the cover of night. It is now in broad daylight for all to see. The Jewish rift is even brought before the Roman Governor Pilate. Pilate's verdict goes against all evidence and any sense of justice. The anger of the mob and the cowardliness of the disciples portray the worst of humanity. Down the street Christ is led, blood dripping from his back, arms, legs, and head. Outside of town the cross is stood up straight and locked into place. The only thing uglier than the bloody body on the tree was the nastiness of the mockers who passed by the execution.

The Israelites knew bloody. Their history was a violent one, and their religious scene was also stained with blood. The Passover meal just completed had to do with blood, lamb's blood. The blood of the temple, only yards away, was so profuse that the stench of death must have always been in the air. Little did the passersby know that the sacrifices on the east side of Jerusalem would be rendered needless because of the sacrifice they so carelessly passed by on the western slopes of Zion.

They were jaded to bloody scenes, but this death was different. This sacrifice was special. This blood was better. The cross is not only the culmination of the story of Christ, it is the culmination of Israel's story. The temple's flow of blood would soon cease as the blood of Christ was shed. He is the Lamb of God who takes away the sin of the world. He is the scapegoat that takes the sins outside the city walls. No longer are the sacrifices of animals needed to foreshadow the real deal. Here he is, the Messiah. Behold the Lamb of God!

So instead of mocking the crucified (Matthew 27:39), instead of weeping in depression and despair as did the women along the way of sorrows (Luke 23:27), instead of turning away from the macabre in a vain attempt to hide the harsh reality, we sing John's prophetic song (John 1:29), the *Agnus Dei* (the Lamb of God). And the earth shakes, the graves open, and the temple curtain tears in two. Man now has access to the Father via Christ. This was also a huge turning point in history. The doom of Jerusalem and the rise of Christianity were about to occur. No wonder we sing the *Agnus Dei* with a heavier tune than the heavenly melody of the *Sanctus* it followed.

Distribution

"The Supper is medicine against having to die," is the phrase repeated by many theologians. The Supper is a means of grace. As with the Word, baptism, and absolution, Holy Communion gives forgiveness and strengthens faith. It also provides us with a communion with the whole Christian church and God himself. All within a meal! Perhaps we take it for granted that this is the way God made us. We are eaters. Eating is essential not only to our life but our way of life. Even from our lush garden beginning, eating (or not eating) had a lot to do with our relationship with God. Sacrifices and meals dot the Old Testament. Our own lives are filled with special occasions marked with meals: holidays, birthdays, and anniversaries. Our personal and business dealings are often conducted with food and drink present. We've already talked about the essential place food has within the family. No wonder table fellowship was so important to Christ and the Pharisees (Mark 2:13-17), with, of course, different interpretations. No wonder heaven is described as a feast. No wonder he dines with us right now.

As the Readings were an extraordinary event, so is the Supper. We come into close contact with our Savior. We come to a dinner where Christ is both host and meal. He is in our mouths—you can't get more intimate than that! It is obvious that this close of a connection with Christ gives us salvation or the opposite (1 Corinthians 11:27-30). Don't let this pass without holy awe. We hear, touch, and taste the Divine. For the ancient Israelites this was an impossibility. No one can see God and live; Moses had to turn from his glory (Exodus 33:19-20). This is unthinkable for all other religious people in the world too. For God to become man, to be present in such a cheap meal, to lower himself so much—it is absurd! Plato and other philosophers separate the spiritual and physical, often relegating the physical to the category of evil. Mystics must reach into heaven to grab the divine. Allah remains aloof and fatalistic.

It is not that the true God has changed since the time of the twelve tribes of Israel. His glory remains untouchable to us. It is for this very reason that he hides himself (Isaiah 45:15). He hides himself so that he may be revealed. In the manger, on the cross, in our ears and in our mouths, he is the hidden God revealed to us. This hidden, yet to be revealed God is what separates Christianity from every other religion. It is his sacrificing love for us. Here we see the heart of the gospel; we couldn't reach him, so he comes to us.

As the story of Christ continues to unfold, we find ourselves in a room with closed windows and locked doors (John 20:19-29), in a small town seven miles outside of Jerusalem (Luke 24:13-35) or on a beach in Galilee (John 21:1-14). We find ourselves dining with our living Lord. To state the obvious, if he eats, then he is alive. This was the amazing proof Jesus gave to the Doubting Thomas, the fearful hikers, and the tired fishermen. Now we come to his table to have our Easter experience. He's alive. And if he's alive that means he is the victor over death and so are we because we are baptized into his death and resurrection (Romans 6:3-6). "Touch my wounds," said Christ to the Doubter. "Take and eat," he says to us doubters. Holy Communion is our Easter experience with our living Lord.

Nunc Dimittis

There is perhaps no better choice for a post-communion canticle than the *Nunc Dimittis* (Now, let us depart). There are a few other post-communion songs sung in the church, but Simeon's song fits so well. Simeon was a faithful Jewish man who was promised a peek at the Messiah before he died. When Simeon held the forty-day-old Christ in his arms outside the temple, he could not help but play the role of a poet. "Sovereign Lord, as you have promised, you now dismiss your servant in peace. For my eyes have seen your salvation, which you have prepared in the sight of all people, a light for revelation to the Gentiles and for glory to your people Israel" (Luke 2:29-32).

He was ready to die and so are we. We have seen our salvation. We had him in our mouths and ears, in fact. What more do you or I need? Nothing. So, with Thomas we boldly sing. It would be okay if a car jumped the curb on our way out of life and struck us dead. We have heaven.

Vocational Prayer

There are several post-communion prayers. They sum up the day's saving activities, especially the holy meal just eaten. They also serve another purpose. The best post-communion prayers have a vocational feel to them. Not only do they look back to the foolishness of the cross, the lowliness of a King riding a donkey and the physicality of the Virgin's baby, but they also look forward to a Christian's vocation in life. Note the similarities. This is how God operates, through physical means: the means of grace and the masks of God.

The means of grace and the masks of God cross paths at the Divine Service. Sunday mornings are for receiving. All the other days are for worshiping. We are living sacrifices (Romans 12:1). Our worship does not conclude with the closing hymn on Sunday morning. There is no vast void between our religious life and our regular life. We are not split personalities, pious on Sundays and rebels during the week, although an outsider might wonder. We offer our whole lives as a living sacrifice to God. Of course, we remember the scene Jesus painted for us of the Last Day (Matthew 25:31-46). We serve others. Our love goes to our neighbors, not directly to God.

So, our prayer is that the love placed into our mouths may work in our hands to love others and that the peace which came into our ears may come out of our mouths to give hope to others. We are recharged on Sunday so that we can get to work during the week. We get so much love on Sunday that it cannot help but be given out during the week. It overflows. Think of the flow of love like water. It comes rushing down from heaven above to earth below. We cannot make water flow up. That's impossible. We can redirect water, however. The love of God flows to us and then to others. It is never really about loving God as much as it is about loving our neighbors. This is the true love of God. We can never please him anyway—he demands perfection. Jesus already took care of pleasing the Father in our place anyway. This is what Luther pointed out to the corrupt monasteries of his day, freeing people from the crippling worry of trying to please a wrathful and demanding God. Our love doesn't need to be used to please God; it is free to love our neighbor. This is a lesson we have not always taken to heart. The father spending time with his kids is just as pleasing as serving at church. We don't need to make more work at church to feel "spiritual." Changing dirty diapers is just as divine.

Of course, the love we receive comes out of a battered image of itself. Our sinful nature dilutes and corrupts this love, so it comes out of us looking pale and sick. Still, we are the masks of God. He works behind the garbage man in order to keep the world clean. He orchestrates the farmer, deliverer, and grocer in order to keep the world fed. He uses teachers and principals in order to teach our children. There is no useless occupation. There is a divine aspect to all of them. In this way, he lifts humanity to a "startling degree."[20] We'll be back next Sunday to compare our weekly report card with the Ten Commandments. It won't be pretty, but still, we are the masks of God.

Benediction

We are now ready to leave the church building. We have said, "It is okay if we die; we're going to heaven." We've asked the Lord to turn the love we received into a love for our neighbors. Now we are ready to be his witnesses in all the earth with our words of proclamation and our actions in vocation. It can be frightening as we turn from the Lord's altar to the doors opening into the world. It is a scary place. Outside are the seas that beat upon the ship of the church. It is the devil's playground. He is a mean bully, and he knows his recess is about to end (Revelation 12).

---

[20] Veith, 72.

We stand with the dumbfounded apostles on the Mount of Olives wondering what to do next. Then the reassuring blessing comes from before the altar as if it came from the clouds on the first Ascension Day, "The Lord bless you and keep you. The Lord make his face shine on you and be gracious to you. The Lord look on you with favor and give you peace." Everything's going to be all right. He will be with us "to the very end of the age" (Matthew 28:20). We began with the Triune name placed upon us, and we end with the triple blessing. He is our Alpha and Omega (Revelation 22:13).

We have come to the end of Christ's life here on earth. He is now ascended into the heavenly realms and sits at the right hand of God ruling all things. Yet the angels' and Christ's final words to the disciples direct our attention to two more events. First, the Lord promised to send the Holy Spirit on the Day of Pentecost, and he did. Ten days later, those same stupefied disciples spoke simultaneously to people who spoke different languages (Acts 2:1-13). The same Spirit is with us teaching us all things (John 14:26). The second event is the Last Day of judgment. The angels reminded the eleven that Christ would return in the same way he left. Until that day arrives, we and the disciples continue to be Christ's ambassadors (2 Corinthians 5:20) to the world, and we wait for him to bring us to the rooms in the Father's mansion, which he has prepared for us (John 14:2).

Conclusion

From the Nativity of Christ to his ascension into the heavenly realms, we hear the story of Christ each Sunday. From the desperation of the Israelites to the Pentecost mission, we hear the story of the church. From a prodigal wandering into the presence of God to performing our daily vocations, we hear the story of a Christian. From the cry for mercy to the table of our Lord, we hear the story of law and gospel. From the acknowledgment of original sin to the pronouncement of the vicarious atonement, we hear the story of Christian doctrine. The Divine Service is the story of Christ and his church told in poetry and prose, music and lyrics. By handing us his grace through the means of Word and Sacrament, he also graciously makes it our story. A story that begins with a baptism into him, wanders through this vale of tears he also walked, and ends in heavenly bliss at his table. The Divine Service is more than hearing about him and his grace; it hands us that grace without any strings attached. On any given Sunday Christ gives himself to us.

ADDENDUM A

The Church Year

We have followed the life of Christ from his pre-incarnate hope to his sending of the Spirit on the Day of Pentecost. Along the way we have been confronted with our sin and its nasty results in the world. The Father has answered our cries for mercy with his Son. His life, death, and resurrection earn us a seat at the Wedding Supper of the Lamb we do not deserve. Remembrances of our baptisms have flooded our minds, his Word has rattled our eardrums, and his body and blood have been placed into our mouths. The salvation earned two thousand years ago has come to us right now.

There is a remarkable parallel between the Divine Service and the church year. Both tell us the story of Christ. Throughout the year we are told the greatest story with seasonal changes, colors, candles, flowers, and symbolic imagery. Notice the parallels:

Divine Service	Christ's Life	Church Year
Kyrie	Pre-Incarnate Christ	Advent
Gloria	Incarnation	Christmas
Readings	Life of Christ	Epiphany
Benedictus	Palm Sunday	Palm Sunday
Prayer/Verba	Maundy Thursday	Maundy Thursday
Lord's Prayer	Gethsemane	Maundy Thursday
Pax Domini	Gethsemane	Maundy Thursday
Agnus Dei	Good Friday	Good Friday
Distribution	Resurrection	Easter Sunday
Nunc Dimittis	Presentation	Presentation
Benediction	Ascension	Ascension

| Vocation Prayer and Benediction | Session and Rule in the Church | Pentecost and Pentecost Season |
| Benediction | Second Coming | End of Church Year & Advent |

ADVENT

The season of Advent is a season of the beginning and a season of the end. It is the beginning of our church year, but it is also a glimpse into the future Last Day. For the ancient Israelites the coming of Christ was also the coming of judgment. Old Testament prophecies pointed ahead to salvation. They do not distinguish between the first coming of Christ on Christmas and his second coming on the Day of Judgment. We have the benefit of hindsight and see these Old Testament prophecies as dual prophecies. For example, Isaiah's prophecy "In that day the Root of Jesse will stand as a banner for the peoples; the nations will rally to him, and his place of rest will be glorious," (Isaiah 11:10) is fulfilled both by the many Gentiles who come to the knowledge of Christ but also to the glorious throng in heaven from every nation on earth.

We in the New Testament church put ourselves in the shoes of ancient Israel, who waited for Christ, and look forward to his second coming at the same time. That's what advent means, "coming." Advent is therefore a repentant season. We understand what Jesus said, "How can the guests of the bridegroom mourn while he is with them? The time will come when the bridegroom will be taken from them; then they will fast" (Matthew 9:15). We, like the Israelites, are in dire straits, and it's our fault. We have nowhere to turn but to the skies and cry, "Come, Lord Jesus, come!"

While the Advent season is marked by repentance, it is different from the Lenten season during which we prepare for Holy Week. Recently, the color for Advent has been a dark blue rather than the traditional purple used in Lent. The dark blue is more hopeful than purple, but it still contrasts with the bright white of Christmas.

Wreathes are often used in Advent. Three blue (or purple) and a rose candle are lit one by one as the four Sundays of Advent pass. On

Christmas a white candle symbolizing Christ as the light of the world is lit. Various meanings have been added to each candle. Here are two:

First Sunday (blue):	Prophecy	Hope
Second Sunday (blue):	Bethlehem	Peace
Third Sunday (rose):	Shepherds	Joy
Fourth Sunday (blue):	Angels	Love

Another unique tradition in Advent is the use of the "Great O Antiphons." These short prayers highlight the different Old Testament names for Christ. They are often prayed during the seven days leading up to Christmas.

December 17th:	O Emmanuel
December 18th:	O Wisdom
December 19th:	O Adonai (Lord)
December 20th:	O Root of Jesse
December 21st:	O Key of David
December 22nd:	O Dayspring
December 23rd:	O King of Nations

The church is set up to celebrate festivals after the day of the festival. The Christmas season starts with Christmas and not in November as in our society today, hence, "The Twelve Days of Christmas" from Christmas to the Epiphany. This puts the church at odds with her surroundings. It certainly is not wrong to celebrate Christmas as our society does, but one is wise to heed the wisdom of the church and to reflect upon sin and grace during the month of December. The traditional Gospel Reading for the First Sunday in Advent is the Palm Sunday account (Matthew 21:1-9). Many of our Advent hymns include references to Palm Sunday. As we explore the parallels between our King's humble entrance to earth and his humble entrance to his royal city, we are reminded why this baby boy came to Bethlehem. He came to die for us. No wonder Mary quietly ponders these things in her heart (Luke 2:19).

Christmas

The Christmas season is relatively short and includes only two Sundays at most. The color white breaks the bleak darkness of winter. The Light of the world has finally come! All the traditional carols, flowers, wreaths, lights, and trees help us celebrate the incarnation. We cried, "Lord, have mercy" with Israel, and God answered our call with his Son. Joy to the World!

Many lesser days of the church year fall in the Christmas season. Some aren't directly involved with Christmas such as St. Stephen's or St. John's. Others fit quite well with the Nativity of Christ, including the Circumcision of our Lord, the Name of Jesus, and the Slaughter of the Holy Innocents, which all fall during the Christmas season.

Epiphany

The Day of Epiphany (January 6) is the celebration of the Magi's visit to Bethlehem. It is referred to as the "Gentile Christmas." Only Jewish people were in attendance for the very first Christmas. The Magi's invitation to the table is a special day for all Gentiles in the world. The King of the Jews is the King of Kings.

The Epiphany season is about the manifestation of God's Son ("epiphany" means manifestation). It is during this season that we see him perform his first miracle at Cana (John 2:1-11) and preach his first recorded sermon (Luke 4:14-21). Jesus Christ is being introduced to the world. It all starts with his baptism, which is celebrated on the First Sunday after Epiphany. In many churches the Epiphany season ends with the Transfiguration (Luke 9:28-36). We receive one last glimpse of his glory with Moses and Elijah before we make our trek to Jerusalem (Luke 9:51).

The color white is used for the Epiphany, the Baptism of Our Lord, and the Transfiguration. Green is used for regular Sundays after Epiphany.

Lent

Now that we have quickly highlighted the life and ministry of our Lord in the season of Epiphany, we are ready to head to Jerusalem. Lent (coming from the word for Spring) is a time of deep repentance. The reason we are headed to Jerusalem is because our sins need to be atoned for. There are forty days in Lent (not counting Sundays, which are "in" Lent and not "of" Lent). The number forty has a long biblical history. The world was flooded after forty days and nights of rain, the Israelites spent forty years wandering in the wilderness, and Jesus was tempted for forty days in that same wild land.

Ash Wednesday begins the Lenten season with a sober reminder that "dust [we] are and to dust [we] will return" (Genesis 3:19). It proceeds without Alleluias, Glorias, and flowers. We fast our eyes and ears until the greatest festival of them all, Easter Sunday. Purple is the color for the season symbolizing not only royalty (see the irony of John 19:1) but also deep repentance over sin. Black is often used for Ash Wednesday reminding the worshipper of mortality. The imposition of ashes may occur on Ash Wednesday. Ashes in the sign of the cross are placed upon the forehead of penitent sinners. Veils may also cover all images of Christ during the Lenten season.

Holy Week

Holy Week begins with Christ's triumphal entrance on Palm Sunday (or Passion Sunday). The Palm Sunday account is the Gospel Reading in some places; in others it may be used in a Palm Sunday processional. Children and sometimes the whole congregation process into church with palms in their hands. After hearing of his birth and life throughout the long winter, we have finally arrived in Jerusalem with our Lord riding on a donkey.

The next main event during the week is Maundy Thursday. We recline with our Lord for a feast. This service often starts off the Triduum, a service that includes Maundy Thursday, Good Friday, and Easter Sunday. At the end of the Maundy Thursday part of the service, the altar may be stripped while a psalm is chanted, symbolizing the stripping of Christ. In congregations without black paraments, the altar remains bare during the Good Friday portion of the service, a striking scene.

Good Friday is loaded with meaningful traditions, too many to discuss here. Services throughout the day are often offered, highlighting the events that occurred on the first Good Friday recorded by St. John. The bidding prayer prays for all people according to their needs. An unveiling of the cross may also occur. "The Reproaches" draw attention to the ugliness of the unveiled crucifix as "Christ" addresses his people. A symbolic closing of the tomb may also be heard.

Easter

After leaving church in the darkness of Good Friday, we return to loud Alleluias and fragrant flowers. He is risen! He is risen indeed! The color white has returned bringing joy to Mary, Peter, John, and us. Lilies are a favorite flower used in church because of their beautiful white petals and strong fragrance. Those flowers not only delight the eyes and ear but also the soul. They are a symbol of the resurrection we celebrate on Easter Sunday. As St. Paul said,

> So will it be with the resurrection of the dead. The body that is sown is perishable, it is raised imperishable; it is sown in dishonor, it is raised in glory; it is sown in weakness, it is raised in power; it is sown a natural body, it is raised a spiritual body (I Corinthians 15:42-44).

The Easter season continues with the appearances of Christ. Readings from Acts replace the Old Testament Readings. We hear about Doubting Thomas, the Emmaus two, and Christ's Galilean breakfast of fish. Forty days after Easter, we celebrate the Day of Ascension, when Christ ascended to the heavenly realms after leaving the apostles and us with his blessing and promises.

The color of Easter is white although gold may be used on Easter Sunday since it is the greatest feast of the year.

Pentecost

Ten days after Jesus ascended to the right hand of the Father, the Holy Spirit came upon the apostles in Jerusalem. The ancient Jewish festival of Pentecost became the Christian festival centered around the ministry of the church. With tongues of fire atop their heads, the apostles spoke in tongues that were discernible to the great many cultures represented in Jerusalem that day. The confusion of the Tower of Babel (Genesis 11:1-9) is undone through the message of Christ, the banner around whom all the nations of earth rally (Isaiah 11).

The Day of Pentecost is a day in which we remember the Great Commission. We pick up the torch left by the apostles who become Christ's witnesses in Jerusalem, Judea, Samaria, and the ends of the earth. Red is the color of the Day symbolizing the fire of the Holy Spirit and the blood of martyrs who considered their lives less worthy than the call to spread the gospel.

The season of Pentecost is different from the season it follows. This is the season of the church. The color for the Sundays after Pentecost (or after Trinity) is green. Green symbolizes the growth of the church miraculously accomplished through the Word and Sacraments entrusted to her by Christ.

Many days are celebrated in the Pentecost season. The first Sunday after Pentecost is Holy Trinity Sunday when we marvel at the mystery of our three in one God. St. Michael and All Angels and All Saints' Day are other favorites. All three days use white as its color. The last Sundays of Pentecost concentrate on the End Times as does the coming season of Advent.

The church year, especially in the season of Pentecost, is dotted with Saints Days and feasts of our Lord. Remembering the saints is a healthy reminder of the way God operates. His means are lowly. He came as a poor baby, rode on a donkey, uses everyday things like water, bread, and wine to give us faith and forgiveness, and a fragile clay ministry to proclaim his message. He even uses us in our vocations to care for the world. We see him use cowardly and pitiful men when we commemorate the cloud of witnesses that has gone before us. Just as importantly, we see the weak flesh of men and women forgiven by his grace. If he can forgive Peter, Mary Magdalene, Moses, and Abraham, he can forgive anybody.

Conclusion

There is no shortage of wonderful things that the historical church has left on our doorstep. Volumes could be written about our great heritage, and they have been. It would be impossible to learn all of it. Yet, it is a privilege to sit at the feet of these men and women who for centuries have spoken, written, and sung the mercies of God. We learn from them not because they are so great, but because they point us back to the Scriptures, that is, they point us to Christ. Every year in the seasons of the church, every Sunday in the Divine Service, every day with the Apostles' Creed, we are told the story of Christ. More than that, we are handed his love and forgiveness through his means of Grace, his Word, his Meal, his baptism, and his absolution.

ADDENDUM B

Biblical Basis for the Parts of the Divine Service

Bells	Revelation 1:10
Processional	Exodus 28:30, Psalm 100:4
Invocation	Matthew 18:20, 28:19, Exodus 20:24, 1 Kings 8:27-30
Confession/Absolution	1 John 1:8-10, John 20:19-23, Psalm 51:1-4, 14, Revelation 1:7, Luke 15:18
Versicles	Psalm 31:4, 32:5, 124:8, Hebrews 10:22, 1 John 1:8-9
Introit	Psalm 100:4, Exodus 28:30
Kyrie	Luke 17:12-13, 18:13, Mark 10:47, Matthew 20:30-31, Psalm 30:8, 41:4
Gloria	Luke 2:14, John 1:29, Romans 8:34, Revelation 15:3-4
Salutation	1 Timothy 4:22, Ruth 2:4, 1 Corinthians 1:21, 2 Corinthians 4:7
Prayer of the Day	Philippians 4:6

Addendum B: Biblical Basis for the Parts of the Divine Service

Readings, Psalm, Verse of the Day, Gospel Acclamations	Romans 10:17, John 6:68, Galatians 4:4-5, Matthew 1:23, Luke 4:44-46, Ephesians 1:12, 1 Peter 4:11, John 20:31
Sermon	Luke 9:2, 1 Corinthians 4:1-8, Romans 10:14
Hymns	Ephesians 5:19, Romans 15:9
Creed	Matthew 10:32-33, Philippians 2:11, Ephesians 4: 4-6, Romans 10:9-10
Offering & Offertory	Revelation 5:11-14, 7:11, 19:5-9, Psalm 34:8, Isaiah 7:14, Matthew 1:23, John 1, 3, Luke 2, 1 Corinthians 15:22, Psalm 116:12-14, 17-19
Prayer of the Church	I Timothy 2:1-6, Philippians 4:6, Ephesians 6:18, private petitions: Matthew 6:1-5
Preface	Lamentations 3:41, 2 Timothy 4:22, Colossians 3:1, Revelation 11:12, Psalm 136, Luke 21:28
Sanctus/Benedictus	Isaiah 6:3, Matthew 21:9, Revelation 4:8, 5:11-13
Eucharistic Prayer	1 Corinthians 10:16, 1 Timothy 4:4, Exodus 12:14
Lord's Prayer	Matthew 6:9-12
Words of Institution	1 Corinthians 11:23-5, Matthew 26:26-8, Luke 22:19-20, Mark 14:22-4
Pax Domini	Matthew 5:23–24, John 14:27, 20:19, 1 Peter 5:14

Agnus Dei	John 1:29
Distribution	1 Corinthians 10:16, 11:26
Nunc Dimittis	Luke 2:29-32
Post-Communion Prayer	Romans 12:1-2
Benediction and Amen	Numbers 6:24-26, Matthew 28:18-20, John 14:1-3, Acts 1:1-11, Revelation 19:4, 22:21, 2 Corinthians 1:20

www.ingramcontent.com/pod-product-compliance
Lightning Source LLC
Chambersburg PA
CBHW020102170426
43199CB00009B/370